PRAISE FOR CHARLES NOVACEK'S
BORDER CROSSINGS: COMING OF AGE IN THE CZECH RESISTANCE

"I have been transformed by this honest, extraordinary telling. In Border Crossings *Charles Novacek shows us, through his personal story (told as if we are right there in the room with him) the true face of totalitarianism; he reminds us of the preciousness, the miracle, of freedom. What a gift he has given us—and what a gift his wife, Sandra, has offered us, as well, in making sure that his brave story is here for the world to read. This is a powerful memoir that crosses all borders and speaks directly to the human heart."*

   —JOSEPH HURKA, AUTHOR OF *FIELDS OF LIGHT: A SON REMEMBERS HIS HEROIC FATHER*

"Here is a story that is meant to survive, just as its teller was. I got to know Charles in his later years but only had hints of what is contained in these pages. They are riveting. I was drawn into the best and worst of humanity and, not incidentally, into the history of the West in the mid-twentieth century. Courage, love, despair, a fierce will are all preserved with the help of one who was 'not the love of Charles' life. . . but his last love.'"

   —JOHN KOTRE, PH.D., AUTHOR OF *WHITE GLOVES: HOW WE CREATE OURSELVES THROUGH MEMORY*

"Border Crossings *helps fill the lack of personal accounts of resistance movements amidst a voluminous array of World War II literature. This compelling memoir, written through the eyes of young Charles, shows how circumstances required him to become a shrewd hero. In his opposition first toward Nazism and then Communism, Charles Novacek's personal story illustrates why people sacrifice themselves and their families for an ideal. Intimate, intense, fascinating!"*

   —CHRISTINA VELLA, COAUTHOR OF *THE HITLER KISS*

D1067276

BORDER CROSSINGS

Love is Powerful!

Sandra A Novacek

BORDER

A Memoir

CROSSINGS

COMING OF AGE IN THE
CZECH RESISTANCE

CHARLES NOVACEK

TEN21
PRESS
DETROIT

TEN21
PRESS
Detroit, MI 48211

Peace In Our Time
Words and Music by Elvis Costello
Copyright © 1984 by Universal Music Publishing MGB Ltd.
All Rights in the United States and Canada Administered by Universal Music – MGB Songs
International Copyright Secured All Rights Reserved
Reprinted by Permission of Hal Leonard Corporation

Jacket/Cover design by Kimberly Glyder Design
Interior design by Megan Jones Design (www.meganjonesdesign.com)
Cartography by Bruce Grubbs
All cover and interior photographs courtesy of Sandra A. Novacek
All Charles Novacek artwork courtesy of Sandra A. Novacek

Printed in the United States of America

Publisher's Cataloging-in-Publication Data

Novacek, Charles.
Border crossings : coming of age in the Czech resistance / Charles Novacek.
p. cm.
Includes bibliographical references.
ISBN: 978-0-9854151-0-5 (hardcover)
ISBN: 978-0-9854151-1-2 (pbk.)
ISBN: 978-0-9854151-2-9 (e-book)
1. World War, 1939-1945—Underground movements—Czechoslovakia—Biography. 2. World
War, 1939-1945—Personal narratives, Czech. 3. Communism—Czechoslovakia. 4. Immigrants—
United States— Biography.   I. Title.
D802.C95 N68 2012
943.703—dc23
2012905875

For Mother and Father

Contents

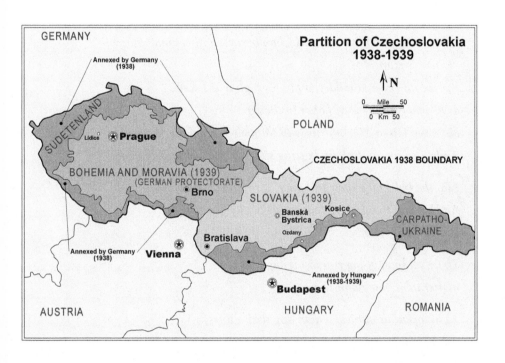

Out of the aeroplane stepped Chamberlain with a condemned
  man's stare
But we all cheered wildly, a photograph was taken,
as he waved a piece of paper in the air
Now the Disco Machine lives in Munich and we are all friends
And I slip on my Italian dancing shoes as the evening descends

And the bells take their toll once again in victory chime
And we can thank God that we've finally got
peace in our time

There's a man going round taking names no
matter who you claim to be

As innocent as babies, a mad dog with rabies,
you're still a part of some conspiracy
Meanwhile there's a light over the ocean
burning brighter than the sun
And a man sits alone in a bar and says "Oh God,
what have we done?"

—ELVIS COSTELLO, PEACE IN OUR TIME

PREFACE

VOLUMES HAVE BEEN written about World War II and the Cold War, but few are eyewitness accounts by adolescents. *Border Crossings: Coming of Age in the Czech Resistance* is a one-of-a-kind story written by my late husband Charles (Karel) Novacek, who as a child and young adult served in the Czech Resistance against the Nazis and then the Communists. Charles died in July 2007, shortly after finishing this memoir. He wanted it published so that one of the little-known stories of wartime Czechoslovakia would be read and preserved.

On October 21, 1996, Charles and I took a leap of faith that astonished our colleagues, friends and families. We married. Charles Novacek was a retired, Czechoslovakian-born engineer/artist and widower nearly two decades my senior. I left my successful position as a small-town library director, sold my picturesque Victorian home, gave away much of my furniture and belongings and moved to Charles' twenty-third floor apartment building in downtown Detroit, Michigan. What to some seemed an act of impulse was for me an act of joy.

It wasn't by accident that the American, native English-speaking librarian met the Czechoslovakian-American widower with the enchanting accent. The lonesome widower contacted a mutual friend (a known matchmaker) with his list of specifications: an educated woman who could be a good companion for travel and a friend and muse to inspire him to create paintings and craft a memoir of his coming of age in wartime. Charles was no Nabokov and I was no Vera, but with humor he told me that's how he thought of us. He had a story he needed to tell and I had the qualifications to help and encourage him.

After our first meeting I felt a strong attraction to Charles. He was charming, witty, and disarming. I had a job I loved for twenty-one years. I was divorced and self-sufficient. I knew I would not be the love of Charles' life, but I would be his last love.

For nearly eleven years the two of us had a good life together. We traveled to many of the scenes of Charles' childhood, the happy places with his parents Antonin and Maria and the strife-filled places of the German and Russian occupations. In the Czech Republic, I met his sister Vlasta; her husband Mirek; and Uncle Josef's wife, Aunt Helena. During these times Charles started to reveal his story. He told me about the photos on his desk of Tomáš Garrigue Masaryk, his hero and the first president of Czechoslovakia, and of his deceased "uncle" Josef Robotká, another hero and leader in the Czechoslovakian Resistance.

Charles never doubted he had a story to tell. He had tried to write the book many times. But he struggled, trying to find his voice while enduring the pain of remembering. It had been better to wait, but now was the time. He wrote and I read and offered suggestions.

The more I learned from Charles the more I wanted him to tell. I knew he had an important story. Like most Americans, I knew nothing of the chronicles of Czechoslovakia. We have been well served by historians who documented World War II, its causes, its battles and the fall of the Third Reich. But few Americans are aware of the Munich Agreement of 1938 and how the dishonesty of England's Chamberlain coupled with the cowardice of the French Daladier sold out to Hitler and destroyed Czechoslovakia. And not many people realize that when World War II ended for the rest of the world, the Soviet troops rolled in and the Communists occupied the remaining Czech territory. In fact, the toll the Communists would exact on the people of Czechoslovakia (and the other Eastern bloc countries) would not be fully understood for several years.

When Charles died I lost my confidant, but I have the memory of his loving eyes, his sense of humor, his crooked smile, his grace and tenderness. I still feel like a very lucky woman even though he's not here—to have been given so much love and devotion, to have learned so much, I could never in my wildest dreams have wished for more.

A few months after Charles' death, I decided by chance to attend a public library program featuring noted Chinese author Da Chen speaking on writing and publishing memoir. Arriving early I was able to speak to him about Charles' life and manuscript and his determination to have it published before his death. Da Chen's message to me was, "He gave you love, now you must give him immortality." These words and the memory of Charles have kept me moving forward to publish his memoir even when the task seemed overwhelming. I am thrilled to present Charles' story, *Border Crossings: Coming of Age in the Czech Resistance*, to be read and preserved as he wished.

SANDRA A. NOVACEK

2012

INTRODUCTION

M ANY PEOPLE SOUGHT out predictions for their futures in the year 2000, but I chose to look back to my past instead; and so I began writing this memoir after graduating that year, at the age of seventy-two, with a Master of Arts in Liberal Studies from the University of Michigan-Dearborn. For a long time I postponed writing, hoping to attain even greater proficiency in English. However, my advancing age set memory deficiencies in motion, and soon I realized that I was beginning to have difficulty remembering certain details. It was a noteworthy discovery. With astonishing accuracy, memories of my childhood through middle age were well preserved in my mind; yet to clearly recall the 1970s and later years I had to revisit and research some segments of my life.

WRITING MEMOIRS OR biographies requires persistence. To tell my own tale, I searched monastery archives, church records, and community documents for information about my forefathers. My life is, quite literally, about to become an open book, and my family will not have to search anywhere. They—and perhaps others throughout the world—may learn from my story.

PROLOGUE

I WAS SEVENTEEN, a dreamer, when the war ended in 1945. Believing that war had ceased forever, I surrendered my weapons to our new police force and dedicated myself to finishing my studies at the State School of Industrial Engineering in Brno, Czechoslovakia.

In less than two years, I realized how wrong I was.

The war for me had just begun.

one

HOW MY CHILDHOOD ENDED

MID-JULY 1948
Prison, somewhere in Bohemia

THE STENCH OF excrement and condensation dripping from rocky walls made the small cubicle feel like a medieval dungeon. I was not a heretic, yet they tortured and beat me every day. Their shouts echoed, ringing in my twenty-year-old ears. "Who are you working for?" When they were through with me, I couldn't walk, so they dragged me by my feet from the first floor interrogation room, down the stone stairs. My head bounced hard on each step, making it ache with numb, buzzing pain; then they dumped me onto a cold floor in a tiny cell. I felt the reverberation as they slammed the rusty steel door.

I began to lose track of time, but I didn't lose the hope of wearing out the nameless bastards. It occurred to me that they may have even been remnants of the Gestapo or the *Schutzstaffel* (SS); these men, new Czech communist recruits, passionately executed the orders of their chiefs, and seemingly enjoyed every minute of it.

Seven years earlier, in 1941, Josef Robotká, my father Antonin Nováček, and occasionally a specialist of the former Czech Intelligence Service, trained me to withstand pain and beatings if interrogated. That year they prepared me to work with them in the Czech Resistance against the Nazis. Now, on the floor of this prison, their lessons were helping me resist the Communists.

In the dank cell, I started to wonder about my life. Such thoughts were also a great part of how to resist and how to recover strength; if one did it well, it could make prison more bearable. I thought back to happier times, when I was younger and roamed through the mountains, paddled about in my old canoe and fished on the river. These times were never to return.

In prison, not only did my childhood end, but also my teenage years, and every day seemed full of warnings about what I might expect in life. I quickly learned to see the world around me in different shades and colors, and knew I had to switch brushes often so I could make strokes that would keep me whole. Self-encouragement held me up, yet fear kept poking at me with increasing force. I had to be alert and remember all that was happening to me. Anything could be useful if I survived.

two

MY FIRST TEN YEARS

*Irresistible need brings out memories
of a childhood filled with fear, anxiety,
and an uncertain future.
They were instilled in me forever. Still,
the firm, tender love of my parents
made me strong enough
to withstand hardships and persecution.*

I WAS BORN BETWEEN my country's two peaceful decades on May 11, 1928.

My place of birth was Ožd'any, a small village near the border that lay between Slovakia and Hungary, where more Hungarians than Slovaks lived; yet the country was called Czechoslovakia.

Babies are usually sheltered; later, however, parents are hard-pressed to hide reality from them. My parents could not keep me from exploring—and sensing many things—at a very young age. Maybe I started turning fortune's wheel on my own, or maybe it was a fortuneteller's incantation that set my destiny moving. The old Gypsy woman—*oreg cigány asszony*—pinched me when I opened my eyes and said to my mother, "The boy you just delivered will always solve his puzzles. He will suffer much doing it, because his first choices will not always be right. Of health problems he will have many, yet he will always recover and will live a long life."

She instructed the midwife to make a knot from the umbilical cord, and to give it to my mother; when I reached age seven, I was to untie it. If I did, all the fortune she foretold would be fulfilled; if I did not, my mother would have to find another Gypsy fortuneteller and have the whole process done over again.

Of course, I untied the knot.

THE WORLD MIGHT have been technically "at peace" between the wars, but political changes were rampant. Was I fortunate, or did my character suffer from these changes? I would have probably developed into quite an oddball, but I was privileged to have uncommon parents who guided me through the tangled web of a perverted and dangerous world. Even now, after three-quarters of a century, I still follow the memory of their lead and credit that for my success on many occasions.

My parents came together from distant countries and conceived me during the decades of relative peace. By the time I reached an age of understanding, major transformations and upheavals were once again uprooting and killing millions. I am a son of war children from times when other wars were fought, and now I carry on the world's never-ending tradition. Will my children have to do the same?

Mother was Hungarian, and Father was Czech; I was a Hungarian Czechoslovak.

Antonín, my father, was born on June 2, 1896, in a village called Tasov, located in southern Moravia. His father, Karel (Charles in English; I was named in his honor), was a farmer and owner of a small beer brewery in the district town Velké Meziříčí. His wife Maria was a homemaker, and brought up my father, his younger brother, and his four older sisters.

The family never left the territory of Číkov, except in 1914, when my father and grandfather were drafted by the Austro-Hungarian government to fight in World War I. Grandfather was ordered to the French front, and Father was ordered to the Russian front. Shortly after arriving at their destinations, they, like thousands of other Czechoslovaks, deserted, respectively, to the French and the Russians, who were then the allies of the Western powers. Forty-five thousand of these men formed the Czech Legion, which after 1918 came to be known officially as the Czechoslovakian Legion.

Russia was then divided into Czarists and Bolsheviks. The Czech Legion fought with their Czarist allies against the Bolsheviks, who overpowered the Czarists. After the October Revolution in 1917, the Czechs, reduced to about 30,000, retreated, trying to get home via the Trans-Siberian Railway through Vladivostok. It was a long and arduous journey, lasting many weeks, and in the Siberian countryside they faced frequent fights with the newly formed proletarians. At last, in 1918, the Czechoslovakian Legion sailed from Vladivostok harbor on the ship *America*, heading to the newly established Czechoslovakian Republic. This is how Father came home; his father arrived home sooner, because of the shorter distance from the French front.

My mother Maria was born on January 8, 1902, in the village of Ožd'any, the District of Rimavská Sobota in southern Slovakia near the Hungarian border. Her father Jánoš Patko was a farmer and his wife Maria Patková, nee Szanto, was a homemaker. Mother had three siblings, brothers Jánoš and István and sister Erzsebét. Mother's native language was Hungarian and I learned to speak it proficiently from her. Slovakia and modern Hungary were both part of the historical

Kingdom of Hungary, a province in the Habsburg monarchy. When the Habsburgs, and Austria, lost power after World War I, a new country Czecho-Slovakia was formed by two treaties between the victorious Allies (Britain, France, Italy, U.S.) and Germany in 1919 (Treaty of Versailles), and between the Allies and Hungary in 1920 (Treaty of Trianon).

Following his military experience in World War I, my father was placed in a police school, and after graduation he was assigned to the police force stationed in Ožd'any. This is where my parents met in 1921. When they decided to marry, their ethnic differences created controversy, especially for the young police officer. Father was a state employee and thus controlled by certain government rules, as well as by biased Czech coworkers. In fact, Father's commander told him outright, "How would it look for a Czech officer to marry a Hungarian woman? Are you out of your mind? See what you can do—change things!" The commander was familiar with the ongoing prejudice among many nationals in Central Europe, and was an older, more experienced man. He liked my father so he helped him work through the predicament. Discrimination was indeed rampant, and I got my earful of it later as I grew up.

Eventually my parents married. My first sister Ilonka was born in 1924, but passed away a few weeks after her birth. My sister Vlasta was born in 1925, and I was born in 1928.

Our one-story house had a large backyard with a barn, and behind it was an open field with a fruit orchard. In front of the house was a wide road that separated it from the Catholic church and the main road that crossed the village. About a half-mile farther along the main road was the Evangelical church, which was built in the sixteenth century. Legends tell of the year 1683, when the Turks invaded Europe, that Zeki Pasha Yali from the Khanate of Khokand fought a Hungarian officer in the top floor hall of the castle on the hill. The sword fight was witnessed by a butler, and when he saw an opportunity for the officer to make an advantageous maneuver, he shouted to him, "*Jobra vágj!* Cut to the right!" The officer did just that, and cut Zeki Pasha Yali's head off. He then stabbed the head onto his sword and with enormous force, swung it toward the village. It landed where the Evangelical church would be built. The legend survived, and many residents believed in the historical significance of the tale of how a patriot helped defend his land.

After World War I and the agrarian reform, a kindergarten was established in one of the large rooms on the first floor of the Ožd'any castle. Mother walked me through there and showed me the legendary hall on the top floor. I was too young to understand then, but later, when I started to pay attention to stories, I remembered the fable as it related to the town where I was born.

Mother showed me the nearby cemetery, where Ilonka was buried. Once a year on *Dusicky* (All Souls' Day) on November 2, like everybody else from the village, we would go to the cemetery, and light the customary candle at my sister's grave in her honor.

I was only three when Father experimented with me riding a horse. He walked the horse until I felt comfortable on it, and then he let me ride alone, only allowing it to walk. Later, in kindergarten, I was admired for my equestrian skills.

Father kept bees. Although my recollections of those years are limited, I haven't forgotten the bee stings, healthy for "us men," as Father used to say.

My mother told of how our dog Sylva saved me from drowning in the sunken water tub in the backyard, which was meant for ducks. Sylva grabbed me by my clothing and dragged me, unconscious, to my mother as she stood in the kitchen.

Naturally, I have few memories from those early years, save what my parents told me. However, when we moved in 1931 to Svatý Ondřej nad Hronom, in northern Slovakia, I was older, and thus have many more recollections from my time there and thereafter.

We had been sent to Svatý Ondřej because the wives of Father's superiors were jealous that my family lived in a prestigious district and that he had ignored all of their injunctions against marrying a Hungarian. Svatý Ondřej nad Hronom was considered the backwoods of central Slovakia, and the envious types thought it fitting for us to be there.

We moved to the second floor of a large farmhouse owned by Mr. and Mrs. Vaník. Two bedrooms overlooked a country road, a neighboring farm, and a five-acre orchard and garden full of apple, cherry, pear, plum, and walnut trees and bushes of currants and gooseberries. Part of the garden was a grass field that was harvested to feed cows and horses. It was also my playground, where I spent much time with the Vaník's daughter, Elisabeth. She was my age, and we attended the first grade together at a school less than a mile away.

Elisabeth played an important part in my childhood. Our play involved everything that children do—including exploration of an intimate nature. It was truly just an innocent touching of each other, yet it cannot be dismissed as if it did not happen, for I believe that it influenced how I behaved later, and how I viewed the opposite gender as an adult. I developed a remarkable liking and respect for the opposite sex; my parents' explanations about things undoubtedly helped to further these feelings. Questions I asked my father about girls were to the point and he gave me direct answers in return. As I became more inquisitive about girls, he told me, "You must never have sex with a girl unless you are married to her."

That command proved impossible for me to keep, but remembering Elisabeth I never touched a girl unless we mutually consented or I was seduced by an older girl. I found that I liked young women very much, and had to be strong-willed to keep my hands off of them; yet I kept my convictions and respected them as Father said I should. I always hoped, though, that the girl would take the first step.

After my family moved from Svatý Ondřej nad Hronom, I never saw Elisabeth again, yet I thought of her frequently throughout my life.

Another playground for me was the river Hron, which flowed about a mile from the house. We would walk in the shallow water or play in the riverside sand. However, it was not a good place to be during a storm.

During bad weather, the safest place was in the kitchen, and it was a fine spot to be in any time. Our kitchen was much larger than the rest of the apartment. It included a dining area with space for me to play and a couch on which our nanny could sleep. A huge chimney was partitioned off, forming a small smokehouse where pork meats, such as hams, ribs, kielbasas, and bacon, hung over a perpetual low and smoldering fire. From the kitchen window I could see a large court area, stables and the barn for the cows and the other farm animals. Grain was stored behind the stables. There was another small barn for wood storage, and in the distance was a deep well covered with a gabled roof with a hand hoist under it. Close to the stairs that led up to the second floor was a large doghouse, and in it were two adorable puppies, my closest buddies.

There were several neighboring farmers, but my recollection of them has faded. One incident that I recall well, however, was when one neighbor fatally cut his throat with a shaving knife and my father, as a policeman, had to investigate the tragedy. The commotion was great, and I received a vivid description of the event from my older sister's friends. Perhaps they didn't even see it, but their words fanned my imagination. They liked to frighten me and, as a result, I started to ponder death. I associated death with ghosts in white sheets flying and scaring people; passing by the local cemetery, I expected to see such marvels, but I never did. In time I began to doubt that ghosts existed, but the fear remained— the fear of something buried in the ground or invisible in space.

Despite my growing awareness of the darker side of life, there was much fun to be had. For instance, I enjoyed skiing with the village boys. Although there were challenging slopes everywhere, we always invented more daring displays of courage and competed among ourselves. My family's home stood alongside the main road, parallel to the river Hron. On the other side of the river was the railroad, and behind it was a huge mountain. Using snow, we built a small ski jump and used it as a springboard perpendicular to the train line. All of us jumped over the train, but only two made it through the locomotive smokestack. I was lucky; my skis were perfectly treated, perfectly crafted wood, while the other boys' skis were improvised from the strips of wood used for wine barrels.

One day my mother didn't know where I was. Then she spotted little boys, ski jumping over the trains. She took my father's binoculars and saw me coming down the hill through the smoke of the locomotive. My father later told me that Mother almost fainted, but she came running to his office, yelling at him to stop us. He knew he couldn't, and that we would find another treacherous activity anyway; at least they could keep an eye on us as we ski jumped.

Every September 28, the whole community celebrated the establishment of the Czechoslovakian Republic, a national holiday. The ceremony took place in the center of the plaza, in front of the statue of the Republic's first president Tomáš Garrigue Masaryk. I always enjoyed the national anthem, but I did not care for the recitation of the ceremonial poem, which was presented by the son of the mayor. Neither my sister nor I were ever selected to recite, although we would have done a better job. Later I understood why; the bigotry against us had already begun to show.

In his free time, Father liked to fish and camp in the hills. As I grew, I became part of these activities, and he showed me how to survive in the wilderness. We used to ride to the river and the hills on horseback. At first I sat in front of him in the saddle, but soon I got my own horse and galloped after him. In the winter, when we couldn't take the horses, we went on skis. Later, when I got older, Father bought a .22 caliber rifle for me. He was very strict about firearms and taught me how to handle them properly. He let me shoot a rabbit or a hare and showed me how to clean and cook them in different ways. I was not allowed to kill any other four-legged animals. He let me hunt ducks and partridges in the valley, but never with a shotgun; he made me use my rifle. We went to the hills together almost every week in every season.

In the hills he knew many friendly *bačas*, herders of sheep owned by the villagers. The villagers paid them a small fee for watching the sheep, and supplied them with living necessities. *Bačas* lived in one-room cottages called *kolibas*, strategically located in the hills. Although *kolibas* were simple and small, they were warm and comfortable in the winter and safer than a tent. Because we were friendly with the *bačas,* we never had to pitch a tent, and were thus protected from bad weather and animals like bear and wolf that might present danger.

A *koliba* had a gabled roof where the smoke from constantly kept fires gathered and formed in a large smoke space. There, in pigskin leather straps, hung hundreds of cheese heads about the size of elongated pineapples; they hung for many months to be well smoked, until they developed thick, hard, brown skins. They were then ready for export all over Europe at very high prices. Nobody in Slovakia could afford to buy that cheese, called *oštiepok*; the government regulated the sale only for high-power exchange. Government agents also occasionally counted the number of cheese heads in each *koliba,* so not too many could be stolen. The *bačas* diligently milked the sheep; their milk was collected in large kettles and boiled for a specific time; then the coagulated curd was placed in white canvas and hung up to drain. The canvas was often tightened to speed up the drainage. After a few days, the *bačas* formed the cheese heads into like size by hand, pressed them into a wood form and hung them from the straps that hung in the smoke space under the roof. They were compensated well for it.

Among all the adventures my father and I shared while in the hills, I recall one rather well. I was walking in the heavy bush, picking raspberries. A little bear cub jumped around the bush to me and surprisingly started to engage me in play; he seemed to think I was another cub. He behaved like a friendly dog, and I didn't see his mother watching us. My father was also looking on, holding his rifle at the ready. Soon the cub ambled over to its mother, as if she had called it, and they slowly walked away. Father said often afterward that he had never seen anything like it.

In 1935, a new film was released, a "talking picture" about a Slovakian folk hero called Jánošik, and I liked it very much; in fact, my mother let me see the film twice. My sister Vlasta had started to play the violin, and after seeing the movie I was quite jealous; the film featured men playing the violin, and I loved the sound of the instrument. When nobody was home I held Vlasta's violin and pretended to play. Then, one day, I noticed that my father had started to craft a violin for me. It had to be smaller since I was still quite young; it was not finished for quite some time. I started taking lessons, and they became a serious part of my daily routine. The violin teacher was a church organist, and he also taught second grade. He loaned me one of his half-size violins while Father was finishing my three-quarter size one.

The movie about Jánošik also had many scenes where Gypsies played different instruments and sang several songs. Before I saw the movie, I had only heard my mother's singing, and thought that, besides her, people only sang in churches. The film opened up a whole world of musical expression for me. From school, passing by a bar where folks drank beer and wine, I heard rough singing in deep voices; I learned it was the singing of drunks. I soon began to distinguish different kinds of singing. Some of the *bačas* had nice voices, and when they sang I could identify some of the tunes I heard in the movie. When I was alone, I tried to imitate the singing and songs I heard in the film and elsewhere.

At the end of 1934, we moved to the neighboring village of Brusno Kúpele, or Brusno Spa, one of the Slovakian health resorts that was visited by international clientele. For Father it was a promotion, though his rank, sergeant, remained the same; he received the promotion because he spoke Russian and Hungarian. The prestige of serving in such a community was significant. We lived on the second floor of the Hotel Boston; a man named Anton Križan owned the hotel.

The spa itself was nearby. One day my nanny walked me to the dance hall there. It was on the first floor, elevated only about six or seven steps above the sidewalk. A large double door was closed, so I peeked in, opening it just a couple of inches, and I saw my mother standing on the podium, singing with the musicians. She looked beautiful, and was dressed in a long lace gown trimmed with white, undulating fur at the bottom; the melody she sang was the *zwischenspiel* "Von Der Golden Pavilion" by Hans Henrik Wehding. Father, wearing his full parade uniform, stood at the window watching her. When she finished, the music continued and Father went to her to ask her to dance. The parade sword flashed at his side as they danced together. I remember crying, though I wasn't sure why, and I watched the entire scene until my nanny pulled me away to go home.

Radek, the son of the hotel owner, was my age, and sometimes we played in the large backyard at the edge of the forest. We didn't spend much time together, but when we did we played rough games. We raided chicken coops, got several dozen eggs, and experimented by throwing them through a window from the barn; in the bowling alley we overheard men saying that one could not throw an egg straight like a stone, because it would always fly sideways, so we had to try it. Radek's father was furious when he found no eggs laid, and whipped Radek when he discovered all the broken eggs near the tree that stood in front of the barn window. Despite all that, we never found out if the eggs flew straight or not.

Soon I realized that I did not really like being around Radek; he was too destructive. His father maintained a clay bowling alley for his guests; Radek would throw a bowling ball on the clay bed, destroying the smooth surface. At other times, he enjoyed breaking windows and injuring chickens with his slingshot. His father was angry with him, and one day he locked him in the underground ice storage as punishment. I finally stopped playing with Radek altogether, because I felt guilty participating with him and not being treated equally; I didn't want to be punished, yet I saw unfairness in it. I was hiding it all from my father, and wondered what he would do if he knew. I couldn't find comfort, so I confessed to him what had been happening. Father did not punish me, and agreed that I should not play with Radek anymore; he was a troubled, misguided child.

The nearby spa had a heated indoor swimming pool. In those days it was nearly unheard of to swim indoors. Father took us there often. Eventually I learned how to keep myself afloat.

I will never forget how impressed I was when my father showed me the spa's mechanical room. The shining machines emitted a myriad of peculiar and intriguing sounds; steam engines turned large steel wheels that pumped something. Though I didn't know it then, it was a steam powerhouse, generating electricity and pumping and heating water. Father spoke to the man in charge, the engineer, with great respect, and said to me that someday I might want to be an engineer. A seed was planted in my mind that day, though it would not fully grow until much later.

The grounds of the spa were immaculate; the benches were painted, the walks swept clean, and the hedges and flowerbeds sharply cut. All of the wooden buildings were well kept. There were balconies and pavilions lined with wood railings, and the multipurpose halls had large windows. I myself particularly liked the public fountains and cascades; a small river, about thirty feet wide, streamed from the mountains and the sparkling, cold water was filled with trout and crayfish. Rocks of all shapes and colors lined the banks of the stream. I couldn't resist exploring.

Beautiful was our time there; yet it was destined to be brief.

HRACHOVO: 1935-1938

One day, Father was transferred yet again. Brusno Kúpele was far too prestigious a place for him, according to the wives of other police officers in Rimavská Sobota. This time he was relocated near the backwoods of Hrachovo, where he would be close enough for them to keep an eye on him. The packing of our belongings was a laborious process, and while the large truck was loaded we lived for several days in other rooms of the same hotel.

The day we set out for Hrachovo, Father said it would be a lengthy trip and we had to behave in order to make it easier on the driver.

The overloaded truck moved quite slowly. All four of us were crammed alongside the driver. At one point, we had to stop at one of the railroad overpasses; the credenza stuck up too high and we could not pass, so Father cut off its top.

It was a very long drive, and the unloading didn't start until the next day. At last, though, we were in Hrachovo. It was October 1935.

While Father, the truck driver and neighbors in Hrachovo unloaded the furniture and our belongings into our new house, I began to investigate the territory, which would be my domain for the time being. I was only seven, and we had already moved three times. I didn't think of complaining; I thought everyone moved as we did. Later I came to understand that a policeman like my father must move from place to place as the police force needed him. His fate was in the hands of the government, and in the government were many people who could influence the decision-makers about transfers. At least I could become more knowledgeable about the country's geography by moving so often.

I immediately started to miss the beautiful, wild landscape that we had left behind in the north. The change from Brusno to Hrachovo was significant; thinking of the high mountains and deep forests with rich animal life, the large river Hron, and my horse was enough to leave me filled with wistfulness. The wild cliffs and the animals roaming in and around them I would remember forever.

In southern Slovakia, the territory was mostly flat. As far as I could see, low hills surrounded broad farms crisscrossing the countryside with chessboardlike fields, releasing a distinctive scent as they stood ready for harvesting. Though they could not rival the mountains I had known, I convinced myself that the hills would have to do for the time being.

By the time the truck was unloaded, I had my territory surveyed. I was quite busy with the layout of the house, the large barn, and an extensive fruit garden of about five acres. The field between our village and the Rimava River extended like an endless plain; I imagined a desert I had read about in stories to be like this. Behind it was a tiny railroad station, a long narrow valley, and on the horizon extended the hills, which were a source for mushrooms, snails, and small game. By then, I was already a seasoned mountain man, knowing what to look for and how to find it. I would not be allowed to carry the .22 caliber firearm my father had gotten for me in Svatý Ondrej; he later explained that someone could have taken it away from me. Instead, I would make a bow and arrows, practice a little, and hunt the small game like a real [Native American] Indian.

I felt restless, despite being as young as I was. Perhaps, I thought, Father would find something for me to do. In May 1935, I had reached age seven; I still had no idea that in just a few months, my carefree childhood would end and the changing times would turn me into an adult, without having the time to truly learn how to be one. I didn't know then that clouds of evil had begun to gather.

Meanwhile, in Vrbovce, less than two miles from my house, I attended the third grade. I liked my teacher immensely; he encouraged us to read and draw with our *lapis* on ceramic boards. My reading skills increased, and by the end of third grade—June 1936—I had read all of the books in the little school library. Then I started reading my father's books, which required greater literacy; I had to read them twice to understand them better. I was incredibly impressed with a history of Bohemia, which had its beginnings in the year 400 A.D., and learned of how its culture and Christianity had come from the Mediterranean.

I had no problems in school. Through the reading I did and participation in school and church activities, I excelled. In church the strongest
competition was in singing; I had difficulty keeping up with the Slovak
boys in that, for they had very good and strong voices. The church sanc-
tuary resonated with the sound of our singing. I discovered that some
kids were affected and even discouraged by the echo and reverberation;
some, however, knew how to take advantage of it and could deliver the
desired quality of sound. One of them was named Paul, and learning
how to copy him gave me the opportunity to compete with him. The reverend favored both of us; Paul because his parents were high in the local
community's society, and me because my father was a police officer.

I liked the Evangelical church because there was singing, and
because the organ had always fascinated me. I enjoyed the Bible school
on Sundays, and the reverend's daughter Katoka kept me interested.
Katoka was an adorable, quiet girl my age, and I preferred to be with
her rather than to play *futbal*, as we called soccer. I did not care for the
reverend, however. Although I didn't know the word then, I thought of
him as a hypocrite. Once when I was hunting birds in the forest, I caught
him having sexual intercourse with a woman from the village. Though
I grew excited as I watched them, recalling Elisabeth, I realized that
though he taught us in Bible school what we should or should not do,
he was violating his own rules. This was the first time I questioned the
church and the Bible, and it bothered me for a long time.

The Catholic parish in the village close to our home was smaller
than the Evangelical parish on the hill. The schools were mixed, and
it didn't matter what denomination one was; one could attend any of
them. Hrachovo and the two neighboring smaller villages had five grades
spread across three locations. Vrbovce, the village south of us, had the
first, second and third grades; the school near the Catholic church in

Hrachovo had the first, second, and fifth grades; and the school on the hill had the first, second and fourth grades. This arrangement was made according to the age and number of pupils in the area in order to shorten the walking distance. In 1935-36, I was in Vrbovce attending the third grade; in 1936-37, I attended the fourth grade on the hill; and in 1937-38, I attended the fifth grade of the Catholic parish. These three schools had only one classroom, so all the grades shared space under one roof.

Our family merged well into the small community. People respected us because of my parents' kind manner toward them; however, we were newcomers, and some standoffishness toward us by locals was to be expected. Since I was only seven, I had little understanding of it then. Hrachovo had about 400 inhabitants, mostly farmers and a few tradesmen. During the corn harvest our family helped husk corn; alternately we went to the farms of various neighbors. Retrospectively, I think our participation was well received by the people, at least in the first year we arrived.

The people with a greater degree of education were two clergymen; three teachers; a notary; five Gobelín tapestry specialists; two brothers Okoličány (the vanishing Slovakian aristocracy); and the doctor, a Russian immigrant, who was drunk most of the time.

A large estate, most of it confiscated by the Czech government from the Baron Okoličány, extended perhaps a thousand acres at the edge of the village. The two brothers who lived there, the only heirs of the Okoličány estate, resided in the large palace, which was slowly falling into disrepair. The government had taken almost all of it and let them have just a small living space, some small stables, and a barn.

Through my mother we became acquainted with them. The Baron started to teach me fencing, and we frequently went riding and explored the territory around Hrachovo. By then I was an experienced horseman.

The Baron was also an enthusiastic skier, and because I could keep up with him even better than his younger brother, he liked to have me with him in the hills.

My interest in the natural world expanded. In the park of the Gobelín school grew many mulberry trees, which we targeted not only when the fruit ripened, but also to collect leaves to feed our silkworms. An entrepreneur from a large city organized many locations throughout the country where mulberry trees grew, recruited children interested in earning money, trained them, and gave each child a four-foot starter tray of worms, which some of us enlarged to additional trays. I needed many mulberry leaves to feed my silkworms. When the worms matured, they attached themselves to the branches I had placed in the trays and began to form cocoons. This process lasted a few days. I had to pay close attention and make certain to ask Father to place all of the cocoons on a pan at just the right time; they were to be baked in the oven, because the worms inside had to be killed to stop them from transforming into silk moths. Such a transformation would cause the creatures to eat through their cocoons and cut the continuous silk fiber, making it useless. The same man who brought us the starter trays came to the Gobelín school to collect the cocoons from the village children and to pay us for them. I produced about two pounds of cocoons and additional worms to continue the production. I received about 30.00 crowns; before World War II, one American dollar was equal to about 5.00 crowns in Czechoslovakia.

The school I attended in Vrobvce, which I could only reach on skis during the wintertime, was a one-story house of about forty by ninety feet. Inside, and facing the village road, was a classroom that took up about half of the house. A small collection of sixty books separated the classroom from the teacher's quarters in the back of the house. It was a structure with a low ceiling, perhaps not more than seven feet high, so the walls offered little space to hang teaching materials like the alphabet and the multiplication tables. The toilet was in the backyard, surrounded by a playground.

Inside, the first, second, and third graders were arranged from left to right and taught by one teacher; there were about ten pupils in each grade. The room had two small windows that flanked a blackboard and two windows facing the road. In winter they were frozen solid with frost and ice, so the only illumination came from two pull-chain electric bulbs. A single, large tile Dutch stove heated the room. Our bench seats were cracked rough wood, and the writing surface was a narrow board that was just as rough.

Between our classroom and the neighboring house, close to the road, was a small steel frame structure that held up a village bell, which was rung three times a day—at 6:00 a.m., noon, and 6:00 p.m. It was my job to ring the bell at noon six days a week. I always rang it proudly and on time. One day, however, I failed to balance the rope properly and my bell sounded just on one side, which was the fire alarm signal for the village. Luckily, the teacher stopped me in time, before anybody in the village noticed it too much. That was the last time I was allowed to ring the bell.

Shortly after we had arrived in Hrachovo, the Spanish Civil War began to rage, involving not only Spanish adversaries, but also the Germans and Russians, who used the hostilities to test their weapons on the innocent. I noticed that my parents were very worried, for they had heard much talk about the war.

When my father explained what civil war was, I became frightened and began to associate war with death and with the ghost stories my sister's friends had scared me with in Svatý Ondřej. I kept thinking about what Father said, and one day I asked him whether a civil war could ever happen where we lived. He encouraged me not to worry about it, because World War I had been fought to prevent any more wars in the future, and therefore, he said, I would never have to fight in any war. The war he had fought in was the last one. Despite how encouraging this sounded, I felt the discontent of the people in the village, and it made me think about the violence among the boys, and especially of the discrimination against my friend Etelka and me because we were not Slovaks. Etelka was younger, but I became aware of her when the Slovak kids teased her because she was Hungarian. I started to spend more time with her, and for the first time I was able to speak Hungarian with someone besides my mother.

My parents had even more to be concerned about that year, for our doctor found a small lesion on my lungs, indicating that I may have been exposed to tuberculosis. An x-ray confirmed the doctor's suspicion, and suddenly I was the center of everyone's attention. The cow whose milk I had been drinking was tested, my diet was restricted, and I was sent to a special Tatra Mountains sanitarium, where many children were under observation and medical treatment. I was there for two months, having much fun in the surrounding woods, hills, and mountain streams despite my illness. I would never forget the Tatras, because there, even more than in Svatý Ondřej and Brusno Kúpele, I discovered the endless fascination of the Slovakian mountains. Under the supervision of a medical team, we camped in the high hills for several days at a time, and I became acquainted with the territory where years later I would perform important tasks for my father during World War II resistance activities.

I was told that the mountain air cured me; the calcification of the lesion on my lungs was influenced by the healthy environment and good food. By the end of August I returned home fully cured.

I became busy playing the violin my father had made for me. In addition, and to ensure that I did not have any time for nonsense, my activities were expanded in many other areas. I traveled to Hungary, Romania, Bulgaria, and Poland with my mother, to visit her friends and went with my father to Yugoslavia. We traveled mostly by train, or in a one-horse buggy if the distances were relatively short. Often Mother took me with her to Rimavská Sobota, our district town; to Ožd'any, where I was born; and to Fil'akovo and Lučenec.

We also visited the Gypsy encampments on horseback. I enjoyed visiting the camps, for the Gypsies were very nice to me. Whenever we arrived, women grabbed me from the horse, held me, and passed me around from one to another. There was always much laughter, and they prepared good food for us on the open fire. I remember well how much they adored my father. Perhaps this was because he treated them fairly, unlike many others in the community. Most folk did not like Gypsies, and complained that the nomads stole chickens and produce from the fields.

I did not understand why there was so much animosity toward the Gypsies until I became involved in a dispute over a chicken that had gone missing from a neighbor's home. A Gypsy passing through the village was accused of stealing it. When I heard the entire hubbub about it, I felt very ashamed, for it was I who had killed the chicken; a stray arrow, shot with my bow, had pierced it. After I shot the chicken I disposed of it, because the arrow stuck in it would prove what I had done. After the Gypsy stood accused, I ran to the station to tell my father what really happened. He then paid the farmer five crowns, released the Gypsy and also gave him five crowns, and I got my punishment; it wasn't too severe, since my father was actually proud of me for telling him the truth of the matter. However, the farmer was not happy about the Gypsy getting off so easily; although I was actually the guilty party, he wasn't angry with me and still wanted to convict the poor Gypsy.

When there were no Gypsies around, the villagers often turned and picked on my friend Etelka and me. Later I understood why this behavior toward us started during those years: Etelka was Hungarian and I was a Czech, regardless of the fact that we had both been born in Slovakia. We, along with Gypsies and Jews, were considered foreigners, and perhaps enemies. These sentiments heightened as World War II approached.

Enthusiastic Slovaks, swayed by the new pro-German government, created a Fascist organization called the Hlinka Guard, which promptly began the "cleansing" process of getting rid of Czechs, Hungarians, Gypsies, and Jews, in that order.

Prior to being forced elsewhere, I found myself at a personal crossroads, having a hard time choosing between my friends Etelka and Katoka. I thought they were both adorable, and I liked each of them very much. Katoka was petite and very quiet. Etelka, though younger than Katoka, participated more in my favored activities, and I enjoyed speaking Hungarian with her. Katoka was in my own grade at the school on the hill, while Etelka was a third grader and had to walk to Vrbovce for school. It was hard for me not to take advantage of the chance to be with Katoka during school hours, and yet after school, when I saw Etelka, I had difficulty staying away from her. To avoid becoming a two-timer at such an early stage of my romantic life, I would have to decide between the two girls. However, the reverend, who was Katoka's father, solved my problem. My mother told me that Katoka was not allowed to play with me, for her father would not risk alienating the villagers by letting his daughter play with a Czech. The prejudice of the times had wormed its way into every facet of our existence—even the little infatuations of children.

In the days before we were commanded to move, my parents frequently visited a Professor Ženatý. My sister Vlasta and I enjoyed going there with them. Professor Ženatý was an old Austro-Hungarian aristocrat who lived on his much reduced estate in a beautiful villa near Lučenec. We loved the nearby riverbanks, which were covered with lush vegetation and surrounded by woods. My sister and I often stayed there for several days during vacations, so I became well acquainted with the layout of the villa and the forests. The professor's housekeeper was particularly attentive to us, since the large household had no children, and she was lonely because the professor was often away, lecturing in history at the Rimavská Sobota Gymnasium. The professor loved us like his own children. We loved him also, and when we were all separated after 1938 due to the Germans breaking up Czechoslovakia and pitting the small countries against one another, we missed him dearly and were very concerned for his safety. At the time, I never dreamt that my contact with the professor and his territory would become enormously important for me in the future, and would impact the outcome of a life-and-death conspiracy.

Besides all this and the important (so I thought) events in my love life during fourth grade, I went through remarkable training in many disciplines. My teacher was an organist and a violinist, so singing and playing the violin became meaningful learning experiences under his direction. He was very dedicated to teaching me all he knew. I was the only one in the village who had a violin, and by then I had already overcome my musical growing pains. Because I could play the violin and knew how to read music, my teacher liked to have me sing as well.

He was not like the reverend; he wasn't concerned about alienating the villagers.

My teacher also knew how much I wanted to learn to paint. I wanted to copy his work and I felt I could do it. Even now I can still see, in my mind's eye, the image of the oil painting hanging in the classroom. Later, when I was able to get supplies, I drew upon that memory, replicating its mountain in the background of the painting.

Vlasta, three years older than I, attended school in Rimavská Sobota, the district city. She studied Latin and French in school, and these fascinated me when she practiced them at home. She did not like my interference when I tried to repeat expressions after her, but she couldn't keep this song from me:

Gaudeamus igitur
Juvenes dum sumus.
Post jucundam juventutem,
Post molestam senectutem,
Nos habebit humus.

[Let us rejoice therefore
While we are young.
After a pleasant youth,
After a troubling old age,
The earth will have us.]

I could sing it better than she after I dug up the words from her papers when she wasn't home.

Vlasta commuted by train to her school, where she had to be in strict attendance. Once there was a huge storm, and the field between our house and the railroad station flooded for several days. Early in the morning, Father carried Vlasta to the station on his back, and he did the same in the afternoon when it was time for her to return home. The river Rimava rose over nine feet, and destroyed the only bridge leading to the rail station. Two weeks later, when the river receded, Father organized the village men to build a new bridge. It was amazing how the men managed to build, with only primitive tools, a solid wooden structure strong enough to support even heavily loaded wagons pulled by horses or oxen.

I viewed the whole thing intently. Men went to the forest, cut down trees, and chopped off the branches. The straight, cleaned timber was loaded on wheels with improvised cranes made of ropes and pulleys, delivered to the river, unloaded, and set up on low wood supports. I saw two men with wide side-blade axes chopping the trees into straight beams of various sizes and length, following the snapped chalk line. While other men continued to bring timber from the forest, Father and the carpenters constructed a high, massive tripod that had a double pulley on top to lift a heavy, round log with a hole in its center. Through the hole went a smooth steel rod that guided the enormous log—the hammerhead, a primitive pile driver being lifted repeatedly by three men to drive down carefully shaped piles for the center support of the bridge. It took some time to get the center support ready before the men moved the pile drive tripod to the riverbanks on both ends of the bridge and drove in more piles for the end supports. I observed how the men reinforced the round tops of the piles with steel bands, made tight to prevent splintering from the heavy hammerhead.

This entire process made a remarkable impression on me. I stood in awe as I watched the design and creation of the structure and the teamwork of the men making my father's ideas a reality, and I almost felt as if a spark had been kindled within me. Almost half a century later, when I would supervise the construction of the People Mover in Detroit, I compared the Detroit columns and steel piles to the piling in Hrachovo, and I remembered my father and his men building that bridge.

In late 1937 the noteworthy bridge erection ended, and in May of the following year I reached ten years of age. At around the same time, the general mobilization of Czech armed forces was declared, and an unforgettable episode changed both my character and my feelings toward my father.

In the middle of the night, I was awakened by loud knocking on the bedroom window. Father was speaking to someone through the window, and my mother was crying. Father was ordered to report to his station to assume command of a small detachment formed by men of the village and the surrounding farmsteads. Mother pleaded with him,

"Don't go, you will be killed."

Father's voice, too ominous to forget, replied in Hungarian,

"*Elsö a hazám és azután te*—My country comes first, then you."

He left the house fully dressed and armed. Later, at the breakfast table, Mother explained that we were at war, and Father had to go to the border, to the front, to take command of his unit.

Despite all of this, I went to school as usual—the fifth grade now, just two houses from where we lived in the Catholic parish.

There were no classes; we just sat around and waited for the teacher to come. Suddenly, we heard a loud commotion in the street. We ran out, and as we reached the street several trucks loaded with men from the village drove by. Our fathers were going to defend the Republic. I caught sight of my father on the last truck; he waved to me, and I suddenly felt as if I would never see him again. What my mother had said at the breakfast table began to take hold of me, and I grew terrified. I fell into a nearby ditch and cried as the trucks headed south toward the Hungarian border. I had heard much talk about civil wars and revolutions during the previous year, but the moment I saw my father on that truck was a turning point. It left a lasting torment in me, which returned to my mind frequently in the years ahead, when I was in trouble.

One rainy day after Father's departure, we sat in the kitchen at the window facing south and talked about what would happen to us. Suddenly a loud military field truck passed by, pulling a short Howitzer cannon.

It stopped about five hundred yards away on a small hill. The soldiers unhooked the cannon and lodged it in the ground facing south toward the enemy. Their tanks, I thought, would come from there on the road from Vrbovce, where my old school was. Both sides of the road were swampy, where tanks could not pass. The cannon had been strategically located to cover the road. I realized quickly, though, that the enemy tanks would shoot at the cannon, miss it, and get our house instead. I took an umbrella and went to see the setup on the hill.

My observations were accurate, so I told the lieutenant in charge,

"I do not care for your setup, for it is obvious what would happen to my house in the event of an attack."

The soldier laughed at me, but a few days later, when my father came to visit from the front and spoke with him, he agreed and moved the cannon farther to the west, so our home would be safe.

For a long time we lived in fear, and there were many events I didn't fully understand until later, when my mother and father explained matters as the war evolved.

We did not know where Father was; we heard he was at the border guarding against the Hungarian invasion of our Republic. At that point, the Hungarians were nominal allies of the Germans, like the Hlinka Guardsmen in Slovakia. After about two weeks the excitement subsided, and we were allowed to visit Father at the front. It turned out he was stationed close to the place where I had been born, but in the hills that defined the border; there the Czechoslovakians constructed massive concrete reinforced bunkers against possible Hungarian invaders.

All of these bunkers on the perimeter of the Republic were so costly our small country could not afford them. The reinforcements ran into many millions costwise, and the Allies financed them. I often wondered if the Allies had expected the war; why else would they try to make a safety barrier not only against Germany but also against Russia? I later thought the Allies foolhardy, for they gave away the Sudetenlands to Hitler, areas where the best and most costly reinforcements were built. The Germans didn't have to fight at all to get Czechoslovakia; shockingly, our land was disarmed by surrendering the Sudetenlands, and the Wehrmarcht simply marched triumphantly into lands that had more or less been gifted to Hitler by the Allies. Apparently they thought the loss of territories in Czechoslovakia was a "small price to pay" if outright war could be avoided. However, when Germany violated the Versailles Treaty and marched into the Rhineland, its intention was to make war to even the score for World War I. History states that World War II began when the Germans invaded Poland, but the occupation of the Rhineland and Sudetenlands surrounding Czechoslovakia (the Munich Agreement in 1938) was just as aggressive. In 1941, the "Pearl Harbor infamy," as President Roosevelt called it, left in my mind questions and suspicions about Japan's maneuver to destroy American naval forces, which prompted the United States to enter the war. While Russia was suffering unspeakable casualties from the Wehrmacht, the Allied help was nominal at best; yet if the atomic bomb had been used over Germany as in Nagasaki, most of Central Europe would have been decimated, an atrocity the United States had to avoid. It seemed apparent to me, as time moved forward, that the war was rife with little betrayals, and many solutions were not solutions at all; despite all the battles won and lost, our true war had only just begun—our fight would go on and on.

None of this had yet come to pass. The bunkers had just been created, and my visit with Father at the front was fascinating. He showed me the strongholds his men occupied; if an invasion occurred, they were supposed to shoot the enemy from these bunkers. Many friendly men called out to me as I walked among them with my father; he told me that some of them could not be trusted. His bodyguards were Gypsies and his main communication man was a Jew; he used to say, "I must have eyes in my back and on all sides to guard myself. The Gypsies and Jews are those I know I can trust."

His opinions were very different from those of many of our own countrymen, and certainly from those of the enemy.

My mother, sister, and I returned home from the front late in the afternoon. Mother was still concerned about the men we had left on the border. The following day, as we sat at the kitchen window and talked about what might happen to us, the rain started, seeming to echo our dark inner mood. Our life changed into a constant worry and soon this turned to almost palpable fear.

My schoolmates had never been too friendly, but now they became downright violent. I was beaten up and abused frequently. Etelka and I soon became inseparable, joining together in the face of the bigotry and hatred that enveloped us. I once heard her mother say we would be a very nice pair; she meant marriage, but nothing could have been farther from our minds. Etelka and I were very good friends; the violence against us strengthened our bond.

For me, 1938 quickly grew to be the worst year of my life so far; I could not imagine that anything more terrible could happen. My ten-year-old self had such limited experience.

My Slovakian peers became even more hostile. Shortly before we departed, a gang of them beat me up yet again, and I swear I can still feel the hard kick in my rear today; my tailbone was damaged and it hurt for a very long time. My friend Etelka was not allowed to go out; my mother told me her family would move to the outskirts of Rimavská Sobota, where they had a large estate and would be safer.

Events in the following weeks became quite sad for our nation. Our military forces were recalled and the Sudetenlands permanently cut from our traditional territory.

When the Germans occupied Czechoslovakia, they separated it into the Protectorate of Bohemia and Moravia, and Slovakia. The army was disbanded, and everything fell under the control of the Germans. This made us part of the Grossdeutsches Reich. Our parents understood what had happened then, but we children didn't comprehend the whole tragedy until later.

In October 1938, we were officially expelled from Slovakia to Náměšt' nad Oslavou in Moravia, where Father belonged, according to his birthright. Father came home with just enough time to pack. The authorities assigned us a railroad cattle wagon for our belongings. It took Father several days to have it all loaded, and we were told it would take several days, perhaps weeks, to travel to Náměšt' nad Oslavou. We were permitted to board a passenger wagon heading to Moravia; we traveled a whole day. Although we were assigned a separate compartment, Father instructed us not to speak of current events at all. We obeyed without questioning him, for we knew something very serious was happening. The fear of the unknown and the presence of spying eyes and prying ears had begun. Though the ride to Náměšt was uneventful, we were anxious about what each hour would bring. At large stations we noticed German police and sometimes the conductor was accompanied by a German secret service agent. I became sensitive to the fact that we were beset by danger. For us, the war that was never supposed to happen began.

As we rode, Father told me many things about his years as a Russian prisoner of war. Learning about Russia and its history, I began to understand why my father might be considered a threat to the Germans; his past made him an enemy of anything German. When we arrived in Náměšt, Father was demoted by the new regime of the German Protectorate. His salary was cut; shortly after that, he was fired and eventually he would be denied even his pension.

For me, 1938 ended in fear, uncertainty, and pitiful encounters in the fifth grade. My unschooled thoughts started to sort out the events around me, but I was not mature enough to curb feelings of sadness, deep remorse, hurt, and even shame. In Slovakia I had been kicked because I was Czech or Hungarian—whichever applied at the time—and in Moravia I was kicked because I was Slovakian or Hungarian. I was learning Czech, yet I needed to follow the fifth grade program of study and my lack of language skills made it beyond challenging. My own war began to escalate.

In 1935, the seven-year-old child had asked his father: "Daddy, what is a civil war? Could it happen here?" That child compared Spain to his own country, as if he somehow knew people were the same everywhere and any nation could be subjected to the horrors of war. He evaluated his chances of survival, knowing that in war anyone could die. It did not matter how he discovered the truth about living and dying; as years passed, these things were always on his mind, taking over his thoughts as the Germans had taken over his land. He remembered killing rabbits and pheasants, and how he searched for ghosts in white sheets but never found one lurking. The more he came to know, the more he questioned.

41

He saw the hypocrisy in a reverend's morality. He discovered among local villagers a growing unrest that was even difficult for an alert adult to detect—unrest that would erupt in revolution, slowly feeding his own countrymen and countrywomen and those in the Hlinka Guard with hate, creating a warlike state where brother fought against brother.

three

LIFE CALLS THE CHILD TO BECOME A MAN

Nature had sheltered me this far;
but now it began to demand
that I stand up and face the music.
I did not know how to dance yet;
I just followed steps.
My eyes were opened when I was born,
but what I saw was meaningless.
Nature had saved clarity for now.

E ARLIER IN 1938, I had been full of fantasies. I played and discovered. I read every book my school had; it wasn't a large library, so even with my father's own collection, I devoured it quickly, even reading some books twice. I was oblivious to what life might become in the future. As I learned and dreamed, I didn't notice the evil coming into my world, and the speed with which that world began to spin took me by surprise. My parents tried to give me everything I would need to keep pace and stay afloat, but we were all just pawns in a high-powered international chess game, in which people became expendable.

The first days in Náměšt' nad Oslavou, at the end of that same year, escalated my realizations and concerns to fears. I became far more attentive to my father's instructions, carefully observed events and incidents that occurred throughout the neighborhood, and listened intently to adult conversations. As I did so, I learned ever more about people and how to read them, and my fear slowly vanished.

I became courageous again, but did not change my behavior in school or the city. At every chance, I explored the deep forests and hills to find places where our family could hide in an emergency. The war was upon us; we just did not know exactly when and where it would strike us. Geographically, our country was right in the center of the impending showdown. I already knew a little about the lay of Europe's land, but solely superficial facts; it was essential for me to know more, including names of the states, populations, and their languages. In those days the world was divided into Allies and Germans, so it was most important to know whose side people were on.

The news was getting worse each day; the propaganda dispersed and enforced by the Germans was misleading, and the traditional harmony in the community vanished.

Father had much to explain to his young son. Most of the time, as I discovered later, he himself did not understand the influences coming from either side of the dividing line. It all seemed to overshadow my own relatively insignificant problems, yet as they blended and rose together, my existence became daily more difficult.

The Czechs singled out my foreign Slovakian accent, and since I was unwanted in what was a beautiful settlement filled with medieval collections of art and history, I became a loner and fugitive. It took me a long time to join the other children and to participate on their terms. Slowly I penetrated into the groups of former "Sokols"—the famous Czech gymnastic association, not allowed under the German occupation but unofficially functioning under other names—participating in gymnastics, tennis, volleyball, swimming, skiing, and ice skating.

I became quite busy with these pursuits, but I always found time to search the forests and cliffs near our house for possible hiding places. I built a cave in the rocks and made it undetectable from the outside; there I planned to store weapons and emergency food.

I thought a lot about survival away from our vulnerable apartment, and taking advantage of the natural environment close by was my main objective. The news of how the Germans had bombarded Poland sounded horrible, and it occurred to me that we could be exposed to the same terrors. If we stayed out in the countryside, away from buildings, we would be safer.

I prepared for the worst. It now seemed likely I would see it.

MY WAR: 1938-1945

I wish I could forget, but I cannot. Events from the past are etched in my very mind and soul. My recollections pain me; still, they have made me who I am now.

My memories from childhood resurface when I think of borders between nations. I now live near one between the United States and Canada, yet I recall other borders not so peaceful or benign.

In 1938, my overall perception of the country broadened, and crossing borders to other countries made me aware of how these imaginary lines separated people who spoke different languages. My father had to stop at the border gate between Slovakia and Hungary. My mother had to go through complicated documentation before we could set off to travel, and only if each piece of paper was in precise order would we be allowed through. Father was not allowed to cross over or go behind the gate at all. He and the policeman or guard on the other side would shake hands over the moveable barrier, exchange a few brief words, and then Father waved to us and returned to his buggy.

There was a thousand-year-old rancor between Hungarians and Czechs. Where I was born, borders had been shut tight since anyone could remember. As war escalated, the grip held upon boundaries became as strong as iron and as heavy as stone.

Our new home on Smetanova Street in Náměšt' nad Oslavou was a two-bedroom apartment with a small kitchen. The toilet was off the corridor, shared by two families on the second floor. There was no plumbing for running water; in the summer, water in a pail was used for flushing, and in the winter, we had to carry a pail of water to flush. We drew water from a well with buckets. The well was located under a large grain depository building a block away. The pails with water were kept covered in the kitchen, and water used for drinking had to be boiled and filtered. Our twice-a-week bathing was an elaborate process in a portable tub that we filled with water heated on the kitchen stove. The two bedrooms were heated with Dutch stoves. One light bulb hanging from the ceiling illuminated each room, until my father was able to mount a more pleasing fixture. The pull-chain switches were attached to each light, and one single power outlet serviced each room. Near the barn we had a lockable space of about ten by eight by ten feet, used to store wood, coal, and potatoes and other vegetables.

Now, without even a small pension, Father needed a job. As a World War I Legionnaire from the Russian front, Father could not hold a government job; he was considered a potential enemy. He found a job as a laborer shoveling stored grain in the neighboring wheat granary.

After a while, the owner needed a bookkeeper and someone to control grain quality; my father was more than well qualified, so his job and pay improved.

We did what we could to make our way in the changing world, and to maintain a sense of dignity and light. In his free time, my father, being a skilled joiner and well trained in woodworking, created remarkable carved objects. He started to make violins and cellos again, and also made a new pair of skis for me. We had some money, but food started to be rationed and we resigned ourselves to frequent hunger. My mother baked bread from flour my father got from the farmers who brought grain for storage. We received sugar in exchange for the honey our bees produced. What we did not have were meats and shortening. Father often joked, "When the war is over, I will have plenty of meat on my plate, and one potato, and after eating all the meat I will throw the potato out."

Corruption among public officials was rampant. Staying alive was the priority for everyone, and the rationed foodstuffs were available only in exchange for rationing tickets, which became the target of dishonest trade. Some employees in the administration embezzled tickets and sold them on the black market, or products would be sold or exchanged directly by the producers. Meats, shortening, and dairy products were major black market staples. Our "protectors," the Germans, created severe shortages throughout the country, confiscating goods from farmers on a large scale and shipping them to Germany or directly to the Wehrmacht at the front; yet they severely punished and even killed people who bought products on the black market just because they were trying to survive.

In June of 1939 I finished the fifth grade. During the entire academic year the children in school had been completely hostile to me, but to speak of childhood incidents seems trivial in light of the unfolding events and war beginning to rage. To forget my troubles I went fishing or played tennis, flew my model airplane, or floated down the river in my canoe, or read and studied to improve my Czech language skills.

I could not ignore the changes in my father's behavior. My mother became secretive, pretending she was unaware of all that was swirling around us; this was not like her, for she was always open and usually knew what was going on. Something was in the air; not just the war, which had begun when the Germans crossed the Polish border, but life as we knew it was changing altogether. It would transform my sister and me from two loving children to two wary adults almost overnight, our youth abandoned.

My father taught me a poem—"If," by Rudyard Kipling. At the time, it stirred my childish soul and made me yearn to be brave and noble, so much so that I memorized it—but how could I know its message would become the cornerstone for how I would live and shape my life, and my refuge when I was oppressed?

If you can keep your head when all about you
Are losing theirs and blaming it on you,
If you can trust yourself when all men doubt you,
But make allowance for their doubting too;
If you can wait and not be tired by waiting,
Or being lied about, don't deal in lies,
Or being hated, don't give way to hating,
And yet don't look too good, nor talk too wise:

If you can dream—and not make dreams your master;
If you can think—and not make thoughts your aim;
If you can meet with Triumph and Disaster

And treat those two imposters just the same;
If you can bear to hear the truth you've spoken
Twisted by knaves to make a trap for fools,
Or watch the things you gave your life to, broken,
And stoop and build 'em up with worn-out tools;

If you can make one heap of all your winnings
And risk it on one turn of pitch-and-toss,
And lose, and start again at your beginnings
And never breathe a word about your loss;
If you can force your heart and nerve and sinew
To serve your turn long after they are gone,
And so hold on when there is nothing in you
Except the Will which says to them: "Hold on!"

If you can talk with crowds and keep your virtue,
Or walk with Kings—nor lose the common touch,
If neither foes nor loving friends can hurt you,
If all men count with you, but none too much;
If you can fill the unforgiving minute
With sixty seconds' worth of distance run,
Yours is the Earth and everything that's in it,
And—which is more—you'll be a Man, my son!

—Rudyard Kipling, "If"

Our parents began to speak to us about what we had to do. First they spoke of survival, but soon their instruction included lessons in how to resist; we were intent upon living and upon doing our best to fly in the face of the forces that would try to oppress us. Vlasta and I were quiet and attentive in our secret sessions with them. Once a week, my father's friend, who was a specialist in the intelligence service and a teacher who also trained professionals, came to educate us about safety in our resistance activities. These sessions included training in how to control or overcome hunger, thirst, and different kinds of pain; how to resist threats and torture that the Gestapo used on children, like continually dripping water on the same spot of the body; and how to handle extreme anxiety felt in darkness or confined spaces, how to deal with fear of cold and heat, and how to increase endurance in walking, swimming, and climbing cliffs and trees. We listened carefully and remembered every word they said. We were instructed very strictly not to divulge anything of this to our friends or neighbors, for we were all in danger. The training went on through Christmas of 1939, and it altered how we related to the conditions around us. Still, we had to keep up appearances, and we did not change how we behaved from day to day in school, on the street, and in contact with local folk.

It did not take long for my parents to make us see the gravity of our situation. We had to grow up fast; our childhood was over. We were taught not to trust anyone, because anyone could be the enemy, a wolf in sheep's clothing. Some Czechs were known to collaborate with the Germans, sometimes to get favors—mostly foodstuffs or privileges to buy clothing and shoes. The Gestapo infiltrated the community to discover political or subversive activities against the Third Reich; anyone deemed even slightly suspicious would disappear and never be seen again. While we became highly conscious of these matters, we were also taught to behave as we always did, as if nothing had happened. As time went by, we became more proficient at this and soon were living two separate lives. In school and downtown we would be the usual kids; while at home, still in training, we would be serious revolutionaries.

In the spring of 1940, my father took me with him to a neighboring town to visit his first cousin, Josef Robotká. We called him Uncle Joe. His mother and my father's mother were sisters. Uncle Joe was a captain of the Czechoslovakian Intelligence Service. He, too, had been fired, and he later became a leader in *Rada* Tří (R3), the major Moravian Resistance group. Joe received us in his garden cottage, and when he and my father began talking, I left them alone; I knew when to do that, for it was expected of me. After a while they called me back in, and we said our farewells and headed for home.

I did not yet know that Uncle Joe was to become an even more important man in my life. Father and he had just made the final revisions for the governing rules of the Bohemian and Moravian Resistance. I had no clue of what it all really meant when my father explained the seriousness of these actions to me; I had just begun to understand why my sister and I underwent all the training and rigors.

"We will not stand idle and be slaves to the Nazis," Father said, his jaw set. "We will fight."

Though in light of the awful things that had already occurred and the growing whispers of even worse, he started to doubt the very existence of God; he also said, almost to himself, "God help us all! At least I know that Saint Wenceslas will."

Given the history of my father's fading faith, I knew things must be serious. He had been baptized Catholic. When he returned from Russia, where he was a prisoner of war for more than three years, he did not practice his religion. My mother was Evangelic, but she also rarely attended church. Still, my sister and I were baptized in my mother's religion and our parents fully supported and encouraged our practices. In Moravia we joined the Czech Brothers, the followers of John Hus; I was a strong believer and a proud Christian. I took classes in religious history from Reverend Ženatý, who shared the same surname as our beloved professor and who confirmed me as a Czech Brother in 1941. He fascinated me with his teaching, and when he saw my serious interest he redoubled his efforts, telling me about John Hus translating the Bible into Czech and how Gutenberg printed the first version. In Kraliçe, the little village where I met the Reverend each week, the Czech Brothers had printed many copies of the translated Bible during the Hussite War; many of these were burned during the Inquisition and the Hussite uprising, but it was also believed that many of them were hidden somewhere in secret underground passages between Kraliçe and Náměšt' nad Oslavou. I organized my friends and we began searching in various caves and passages, but we gave up after we found nothing. Still, for some time, my faith was far more fervent than that of my father.

We were close to home that day when Father said again, "God help us. God help us all."

His face turned red and his lip muscles twitched, as if he were trying to hide whatever emotion he felt. I kept quiet, knowing instinctively how grave our situation must really be. When we reached home, my father embraced my mother, and I saw them both weep.

"I was so wrong," my father said. "We are at it again." In Slovakia, when he had promised I would never have to go to war, that the last war had been fought, he had truly believed this; now he saw with a terrible clarity that he had been direly mistaken.

That evening, after we returned from Uncle Joe's, our family sat in the small bedroom that faced the garden. From there nothing could be heard from the outside, yet we spoke softly.

"Now you know," Father whispered, "why we trained you so much and so strictly. If we are to make it, we must be strong. We must not be afraid, for fear would make us seem suspicious and would give us away. Yet we cannot be foolish either; we must be alert, and constantly vigilant. We all have a job, and you children can do many things we older folks cannot. You, Vlasta, going to school in Třebíč every day, can cover that territory. You will not tell your brother what you are doing or what contacts you make, and you will not know what we are doing here at home."

He paused for a moment, as if to search our upturned faces; apparently he found what he sought, some determination, for he continued, "In the beginning, our primary function will be to keep intelligence agents from England safe and fed. They have been dropped in parachutes in specific places and picked up by me or others and led into the hills, from where they were taken even farther into the cliffs for safety. Sometimes we take them into large towns, where among crowds and many buildings it is often easier to hide. We cannot have radio communication as of yet, so we have to do things the hard way, in person. At all costs we must avoid confrontations with the SS and the Gestapo, and we must stay away from the Czech Police, for we can't be sure what side they are really on and we don't know who they are. Our best defense right now is to appear unsophisticated—as if we know nothing. Your main job will be to keep up with your school assignments; when you have to be absent you will fake illness, and for that you will get a signed note from your mother or from me."

This was astounding talk, and I felt that the need for hiding places was even more urgent. In my free time and in the evenings I had already dug an underground space in the cliffs close to our house. Nobody would ever suspect that location, for it was in a dangerous spot high in the rocks, and not accessible to ordinary people or wayfarers. For my mother and sister I made special access to it, overgrown and camouflaged with heavy boulders.

After the cave was established and stocked, I found another place much farther away from home, just in case the first one did not work out due to its proximity to our house, or in the event that somebody found out about it. The second was larger for more comfort, but it was not as safe as the first; it was more easily visible and therefore more accessible. There I hid two bottles of water, which I frequently changed, a little sugar and honey, some crackers in a tin box and even one bottle of moonshine that I slowly filled so my father would not notice. When I finished, it was large enough for four people and safe storage of two boxes of dry food. There I also kept weapons and ammunition that I was able to steal during our occasional encounters with the Germans. The cave was a dry, covered space that was safe from the wind and the rain, and I thought that in an emergency it might prove a haven for our family.

East of the cave nearest to where I lived, I could see part of the street where my house was, the river Oslava, and behind the river, the railroad bridge. Past the railroad were the hills where I skied, and on the horizon to the south was the small skyline of the city. The area between my bunker and the hill where we hid our English friends was a difficult terrain to cross; so also was the area in which we had other well-disguised places for them, the German territory southeast of Znojmo, considered part of the Sudetenland. The whole expanse was the southeastern part of the Ceskomoravská Vysočina, i.e., the Moravian Highlands, and I was a king in these parts; nobody knew them better. Here the grownups grew to trust me more than themselves.

The Náměšt Castle, the residence of Count Haugwitz, was to the southwest, high on the hill; the old palace housed Gothic treasures, and along the surrounding roads were many full-size stone carvings. The middle school was about a mile and a half south of our home by way of a dirt road; the road paralleled the river, across which Vaclav

Adrian von Enckevort had built a Baroque bridge in 1737. The bridge was decorated with twenty statues of saints and archangels; eight had been carved by Josef Winterhalter, Senior, one of my heroes in the art world. Because I stopped to admire the carvings on the way to school I would often be late.

Despite the trials of the time I still searched everywhere for watercolors and paper. I begged one of my teachers, whom I saw drawing the bridge with pen and ink, for help in getting these things; he seemed to have paper, but the rest of his response was negative and sad, for he could not obtain materials for me. My mother brought me packing paper and I experimented, working with a "fill-pen" that had just then come on sale in the local office supply stores. My father gave me a smooth, thin pine board measuring about twelve by eighteen inches; upon it I stretched the paper from Mother as best as I could, fastened it with four thumbtacks, sat along the shore of the river, and used my fill-pen to sketch the bridge and the castle that stood in the background. I did it at least six or seven times before I began to achieve relative sizes and equivalent perspective.

The view I was trying to capture had already been overused by many other painters, but hiding as I was in the heavy bush I discovered different viewpoints of the popular subject. I had seen many paintings and drawings of it in many different mediums and styles, but never just ink on rough paper. Concealed from passersby, I perfected my drawings; I just needed paints to do them in color.

Around the corner, not far from the bridge, was a small barbershop. In its sitting area was a small table, covered with paper. The barber had it there for his convenience and changed it after a long time, when it became dirty. I asked him to put aside the paper for me and was able to use the clean side. One day I showed him my drawing and he put it on the table, gave me twenty cents for a soda pop, and also a few sheets of totally blank unused paper.

I was determined to find or make my own tools and paints from things I saw in the garden, nearby fields, and on the riverbank. For brushes I experimented with pussy willows; by the river I found yellow, brown, and nearly white clay, which contained some sediments of kaolin. I also experimented with tomatoes, onions, parsley, and red beets. I invented many shades; however, in a short time they changed into bleached smudges which I then tried to repaint, and I soon had to be satisfied with just that. The charcoal I got out of the fire in the smokehouse was quite messy, until I learned to get special pieces of charred branches that were just about half an inch thick; plus, they had to be cherry or plum. As for subjects, my mother was very pretty. I observed her face and wanted to be able to paint it.

Of course, given the way the world was turning, my time drawing and painting was extremely limited. My chances to explore the nuances of love also became increasingly curtailed; I longed for the kind of special friendships I had experienced before, when life seemed happier, freer, and simpler. At some point, however, I met a friend of Vlasta's; her name was Sylva, and I thought she was very beautiful. She was fifteen, a year older than I, and she knew things that I did not. From her I learned much, and I experienced for the first time the act of love in its fullest form. I had not been aware that such pleasure could possibly exist, especially not in the times in which we all found ourselves. The exquisite curve of waist to hip, the fluttering touch of lips in once covered places, the ecstasy of entry, the tumult of the rise and fall—all of these astounded me, and I thought that now, at last, I had grown to manhood.

Such moments of bliss were brief. Somehow, my father found out about my budding relationship with Sylva, and told me all over again what was expected of me as a proper young gentleman. I rarely could see Sylva, and slowly but surely, our lives grew apart; we were not to be. My father never encouraged involvement; life had grown far too serious and bleak. I was ever more busy with schoolwork and, more importantly, with special jobs my father assigned to me.

One day I went with my father to meet men from England. Two had parachuted in at night; we took them to the hills in the plains of Znojmo, in the Sudetenland. Eight of our men met us at the location. After we brought the two paratroopers to safety, we returned through rocky and mountainous terrain to Moravia. Before we crossed the imaginary border between these two territories, we found ourselves confronted by a German force.

It was not a coincidence; we had just begun using our radio to communicate, and they probably intercepted the transmission and were thus now waiting for us. Before we crossed the river and noticed them, they shot one of our men and pinned us down in a small depression about a hundred yards from the river. We could not move; the Germans controlled the field between our cover and the flowing stream.

Our wounded man was dying, and desperately needed water to drink. My father handed me an empty glass flask and commanded me to bring water. I could not believe he was serious; my chances of getting through to the river were slim to none. Still, I knew he couldn't do it, so I had to try. I made it there, but as I returned with the water I tripped in my haste and fell, breaking the flask. My father shouted, "I told you to get water!"

I had never heard him sound quite that way—so stern, so urgent. So I crawled again to get another bottle, scared to death. This time I not only made it there, but I made it back again with the bottle and water intact.

Father noted that there were only two men with one machine gun, but he was concerned the shooting might alert their larger detachment, which would doom us to further discovery and death. He ordered us to stay put and to be motionless. It worked; yet in the meantime, as we waited, our friend died. At the same time the two Germans became impatient, thinking they had killed us all, and began to peek out, leaving their cover. One of our own sharpshooters quickly got them, and we were then safe to properly bury our friend. We took everything that could identify him out of his pockets, and we also masked the ground where we laid him to rest. Then we left for home, saddened and shocked, but unable to allow ourselves to grieve.

The next day in school, I brought a false note from my mother saying I had been ill. I came in time to enter my drawing in a contest; I knew that I would lose, for there were other privileged kids, like the pharmacist's son, who almost always won no matter what kind of contest we had. I did beat him in the string quartet, however, and got the first violin position. At first I wondered about this, but when I sorted things out, I started to understand that nobody wins all the time. At any rate, it was a good cover for us to be constantly involved in school, concerts, tennis competitions, building airplane models, or skiing in wintertime.

Mother herself was the best cover of all for us, because she was Hungarian and thus to the ordinary town folk a foreigner and likely to be a Nazi collaborator—and therefore to be avoided. Similarly, a local noble, the German Count Haugwitz, was a strong supporter of our underground resistance. He despised Nazis, but the villagers did not know that, and since he was German everyone viewed him as a Nazi.

Shortly after we had arrived from Slovakia, I built a cage in our lockable wood storage shed to breed rabbits. I had great success with this, and as the years passed the rabbit families burgeoned until I had three full groups, and had to create an extra cage to make them grow faster. This project of mine became an important source of protein for us, and even my mother helped me to get grass for them. In December of 1941, after America finally entered the war, we celebrated with a stew of rabbit and potatoes.

My father put together a small still some time back, and occasionally he made moonshine from fruit and potato peelings. He ran the distillate several times to purify it, explaining to me that the unrefined alcohol would be harmful to us. When we heard about the United States' declaration of war against Germany, the whole family celebrated with a drink, though we had to do so quietly. My mother wept with joy, hoping America's involvement would bring things to a close more swiftly.

I grasped the importance of the events at Pearl Harbor, and my father announced, "Now it is certain that we will win the war."

On Christmas Eve, Father and I went to get a small tree; instead we came upon a scene that was hard to forget. There was a picket fence dividing two wooded areas; one of the sticks had loosened and bent sideways, forming a large v-shaped opening. A small deer had been caught in it by its hind legs as it jumped through; it must have happened just moments before, as the animal was still warm. My father stuck it at once to drain the blood out and then dragged it to a thicket, where he cleaned it and cut it into two parts so we could carry it home. He did so quickly, since Nazi law prohibited the killing of animals for food. My father's masterly cuts reminded me of our hunting expeditions in the cliffs of Svatý Ondřej just a few years back; it seemed as if far more time had gone by. Silently he wrapped the smaller part in my jacket and the larger in his, saying that the jackets could be washed, but that we had to pack and conceal the meat well so that nobody would suspect what we were carrying.

We shared our prize with no one; we could not trust anybody. We would have been prosecuted, because it was considered stealing from the community forest. The Germans had executed people for less, or dragged them to a concentration camp where they would inevitably meet their doom anyway. As we made our way back toward home, he continued. "This was a miracle. Now we will have meat for Christmas. It will be a holiday like we haven't had for a long, long time."

We did not talk much during the rest of the way back, and as we saw no one, it was an uneventful walk. When we got home, Father did more cutting and sorting of portions for the days ahead while I brought ice from the river; I would have to bring ice every day to keep the meat fresh. Two large containers were filled and locked in our coal bin.

Father himself prepared the Christmas Eve supper, dressing and seasoning the meat well. I was very hungry, yet I could not eat a thing; I kept thinking of the poor animal being caught in the fence. My father noticed, but said nothing. After a few days, I finally succumbed to the temptation of the persuasive smells and ate, but I never shook the memory of that incident.

The next day, Christmas Day, we cut and decorated our tree. The whole family participated in the small festivity. Such times were few and far between.

During January and February of 1942, the temperatures dropped drastically. Trees were cracking apart, seeming to explode, and wild animals had to be brought into shelters to keep them from freezing to death.

We had many difficulties shielding our friends from the elements. They came with special assignments to help us blow up specific German installations, so the Nazi war machine would be hampered. They brought us many explosives and weapons; these supplies had to be distributed among groups throughout the country or properly stored in our own arsenal. The Allies sent several radio units, which had to be delivered to particular locations for operators who knew the codes and how to send and receive messages. The Gestapo was becoming ever more sophisticated, and our radio operators had to change stations, signals, and codes frequently. Later, in 1943, we would be completely prevented from using radio communications with England, because the Germans created an advanced triangulation system that could detect a signal in seconds. For a long time we relied on the shortwave London news broadcasts for coded messages. The Gestapo raided homes to check for shortwave radios; these were outlawed so people couldn't listen to the BBC broadcasts from London. Father maintained a simple setup, just a small piece of wire, which he placed in the back of the receiver between two devices and thus picked up short waves.

Life became more and more complicated, and the London evening news, which always began with the famously ominous first notes of Beethoven's Fifth Symphony, kept reminding us that the war was all too real and the German *Drang Nach Osten*—Drive to the East—was well under way. In those days, Stalin—called "Daddy Stalin" by many—sounded like he might be a real fairy tale savior; at that time, we knew nothing about his atrocities and purges, and our patriots banked on his intentions to save us.

In May of 1942, I turned fourteen and was deeply involved in school. Biology, history, geography, music, singing, painting, and languages, including the Czech and German tongues, filled me with endless fascination. Everyone else hated the German language, but I did not; I redoubled my efforts to speak it well. I counted German as my third language, and the teacher was very happy for me. She was a Czech lady and, knowing German perfectly, had been appointed to the middle school. With my skill in speaking German and my Hungarian mother being looked upon as a "foreigner," our family had an excellent cover for our underground involvement.

One day a tall, strong classmate of mine badmouthed my mother during recess. I did not mind when the tough guys harassed me about my Slovakian accent; however, when this one began to insult my mother I flared up, hit him, and flattened his face. It looked quite bad; even I got frightened, for blood was everywhere. I was ushered into the school director's office and threatened with expulsion. My father was called in. When he came and was told what had happened, he wanted to hear my version and talked to me first.

"For Christ's sake," he asked, "what did you do?"

"He was saying bad things about Mother, so I . . . hit him a little."

"Oh, yes . . . a little! You pushed his nose clear through his mouth! Still . . . I understand. I myself might have done what you did," he said, smiling a bit. "Just don't do it anymore, please."

I was not expelled.

However, only a couple of weeks passed, and a similar incident occurred in the boys' room. This time it was a different bully who refused to stop the Hungarian insults and moved on to saying far worse. Instead of hitting him, I merely set about drowning him in the urine basin. He would be fine after a while, though the teachers and a doctor had a hard time getting all the urine out of his lungs. Still, I thought I would be expelled for sure. Once more the director called my father to complain about me.

Again, Father asked me, "What did you do now?"

"I'm sorry, Father, but he just wouldn't stop with his badmouthing, and he called Mother a terrible name. I didn't hit him, so I did as you asked. I just pushed his head into the urine basin a little bit."

"A little bit! Yes, a little, and he almost drowned in it."

"I really am sorry, but nobody should ever speak like that about my mother. I won't hurt anybody anymore, but stop them from harassing me and from saying the things they do."

My father was always fair, and he told the director to speak to parents about these disturbances; obviously the kids picked up some ideas from their parents and then expressed them at school. I recall, however, not having any animosity or hatred toward them at all; I very much wanted to be a friend to them. After all, I was a Czech just like them; if we couldn't get along with each other in one small country, how could we ever expect to have all of Europe get along?

Our whole nation was in deep trouble; our people were divided; and no one could trust anyone else. There was great hunger, fear, and intense discontent. My parents were concerned about our safety in the whirlwind of the war; daily they reminded us of how important it was to keep our wits about us and to prevent confrontations.

After the assassination of the Reichsprotektor Reinhard Heydrich, all classical institutions were closed in retaliation. Heydrich's assassination has been described as being carried out totally by English agents, but I knew better. A lot of the planning for the act—and the killing itself—was done by the Czech Resistance, but since it occurred in the presence of the agents from England, they were credited for the whole thing. The Germans murdered civilians in Lidice and Ležáky and intensified their surveillance, trying to discover subversive activities. We made a serious mistake by killing Heydrich in Bohemian territory; the reprisals were too awful.

We never confronted the Germans in our territory again, for fear of such retaliation. The Gestapo was everywhere; the Gestapo checked on the Schutzstaffel (SS) and the SS checked on the Gestapo, for each was self-conscious and each felt superior to the other. Both were cruel and dangerous, and terror continued to escalate.

I reached the final year of middle school and wanted to transfer to an art academy, but these were among the schools that had been closed. If I could not get into an accredited institution that was recognized by the Germans, I would have been drafted to the *Technishe Nothilfe (TN)*—the German Black Army, which was cleaning up after bombardments in Germany. The death rate in the *TN* was nearly 50 percent; I did not care for those odds. The only institution open and recognized by the government was the engineering college, and the minimum entry age was eighteen, and then only if one passed a rigorous exam and had a minimum three-month apprenticeship in an engineering field. I was only fifteen and not prepared for a technical field of any kind; for me, to pass the exam would be impossible. Still, my father could fix anything; he simply changed my age to eighteen, using his connections to have my paperwork altered. His friends from the Russian front, professors in the college, arranged my entry exam, and I was accepted into the college of mechanical engineering; furthermore, I carried a certificate of having worked and practiced in an auto shop.

I also had to prove there was no Jewish blood in the six previous generations of my family. The Nazi-controlled government required this for all student applicants. It was easy to obtain information about my father's family in Moravia; I made the trip in just a couple of days, riding from village to village by bicycle and getting copies of records from monasteries and churches as needed.

For my mother's records, however, I had to travel to Ožd'any, Slovakia, where I was born, and search through community records, two monasteries, and the Evangelical church there, which had traditional records of all the people in the Gemer province. When I explained the situation to the church prior, as my father had told me to do, he was very understanding.

I finally found the necessary documents that referred to my mother Maria Nováčková, nee Patková. The family history I saw went as far back as 1767 so the monks could write excerpts from records for me to satisfy the Nazi requirements in 1943. The prior provided me with a handwritten certificate, signed and sealed, that stated clearly that my mother had no Jewish blood through at least seven generations. He dated it all the way back to 1767, so the requirement for entry into the college of engineering in Brno was satisfied.

At the beginning of May 1943, my father ordered me to go to the Tatra Mountains in Slovakia to a very specific location near the Polish border, not too far from where we used to ski. I was to meet a young man from Warsaw, who would give me a paper with a message that I had to bring to the Hungarian border, close to Ožďany. There, I would give the same message to another young person; at that time my father wasn't sure if this would be a woman or a man. The message was from the Polish partisan, who wanted to have it delivered to English agents stationed on the shores of the Black Sea; he was a friend of the rebels in the Warsaw Ghetto Uprising and wanted to send word to the outside world about the conditions of the Polish Resistance. They desperately needed arms and ammunition. Father negotiated with him for the possibility of joining forces and strengthening our mutual efforts against the Nazis.

It took my father some time and effort to organize and connect this hand-to-hand delivery through Poland, Slovakia, Hungary, Yugoslavia, and the Black Sea; he did it gladly and hoped to persuade his counterpart in Warsaw to join.

The timing and the place of the meeting in the Tatras were perfect. I approached the location at the same time as my Polish friend. I was surprised when I saw him up close; he was only in his early to mid-twenties, and wore a priest's collar. We wept as we embraced, recognizing each other as brothers in a shared cause. He spoke Polish and I spoke Czech, and yet we understood each other quite well. It occurred to me that he dressed as he did for cover. Decades later, however, I would doubt my assumption about his disguise, for in 1978, a man who bore a striking resemblance to him and bore a name like my own walked out on a Vatican balcony and raised his hands in blessing on a waiting world.

I successfully delivered the message he gave me to the Hungarian border. There, the messenger was a Hungarian man of about forty years of age, who was extremely happy to learn I spoke his native tongue.

I returned home in four days, and when my father greeted me I noticed a moist glint in his eyes; clearly he had been concerned about my well-being and was relieved I returned in one piece. As usual, I had to bring a note from my mother to school, which detailed how terribly ill I had been.

At the end of that month, as my middle school year drew to its close, we had a frightening experience during a German language class. Without warning, the classroom door swung open, and a tall, brutal-looking SS officer stood in the doorway. Everyone in the class froze. I thought our teacher would faint, for she was absolutely terrified. The man in the door looked over our room and said loudly, "What have you learned in German? Surely you must know something in the greatest language, the tongue of warriors and heroes. Say something in German, now!"

His manner was arrogant, forceful, and bordered on threatening. My teacher could not utter a word; she just gasped helplessly for air.

Without realizing what took hold of me, I stood up and began to sing a well-known German military tune, known as the "Westerwald Song." I did so with fervor, as if there were no greater thrill for me; to emphasize the rhythm of the song, I hit the floor with my right foot, imitating what the German soldiers did when they stood singing.

At last, at the close of my impromptu performance, the officer departed, seemingly satisfied. I jumped up to catch our teacher, who at this point was unable to hold herself up any longer and was starting to fall. I felt great hatred toward that man, not just because he was a Nazi, but because he instilled such fear in innocent people. My teacher later came to visit my parents to tell them what happened, and how proud I had made her.

Our daily routine did not change, except for me working in the auto shop and studying math and physics. My father found an engineering student and hired him to tutor me in these subjects, and also in chemistry. I had virtually no time for anything else, save for when I was needed in the hills to deliver food or to hide someone. That was my number one priority, and I was never allowed to miss this duty.

One day, though, an order came from the government that all students and future students must work in the factory, fabricating war products. There were two factories in Náměšt, one that made casings for cannon shells, where I was assigned, and another where soldiers' uniforms were made; my sister was assigned to this one.

I worked for just two days before I injured myself while lifting one of the boxes filled with casings. I had a hernia, and was sent to a doctor for an examination. He verified it and sent me on to Třebíč Hospital. I traveled by train, alone, for about twenty-five minutes, holding the protrusion that was already forming on the right side of my groin.

The once very well-staffed hospital had been reduced to a poor dispensary; nothing that a good hospital might need was left. All the supplies had been cut or rerouted to the German war efforts. The doctor who examined me said I had two choices: one, to be operated on; the other, to wear a belt with a huge ball on it that would push the protrusion back.

"If we operate, I cannot give you relief for pain or narcotics; I do not have ether. I can give you a couple of shots of alcohol, which will numb you up a little. The worst of it will last for about twenty minutes. We will tie you down so you can't move, and you can scream all you want. Once we start, we can't stop just because you feel pain. What's more, right after surgery you must go home, even though you are by yourself, for you cannot stay here. You should be all right, but the pain will continue for a few days and for a few weeks you must not do any work. So, what is it going to be?"

I put on a brave face and said, "Okay, Mister Doctor—I can take it. Just give me a drink and let's get on with it."

I returned home on the last train, late in the evening, and somehow managed to walk home from the station; I had to make frequent stops. Nobody in my family knew what had happened; they thought I'd been busy in the auto shop. My mother and father just looked at each other when I showed them the bandage, which held me up straight.

The doctor's certification freed me from the forced labor and I was thus able to spend more time studying; however, I could not go up into the hills for about twenty days, so my father and sister filled in for me.

Though war raged everywhere, I managed to become accustomed to the big city and my new school. As far as my studies were concerned, however, I was in way over my head. My few weeks of crash tutoring gave me just a short overview of what engineering would be about; for me, the program was overwhelming. Most of my colleagues were men over twenty; some of them were graduates from schools that had been closed after Heydrich's assassination. However, professors knew who I was and were helpful in keeping me afloat; they did it for my father's sake, and put forth extra effort to make an engineer out of me. It was a challenge for them, but they knew that if they let me go, I would immediately be drafted into the Black Army. I studied as hard as I could, and my father retained the tutor so I could overcome hurdles as they arose.

Meanwhile my important duties in the hills had to go on, and I was also assigned as a contact to Captain Zdeněk Žárský, who had a shop in Brno. We transferred messages in person; they could not be sent by radio, as it was too risky. My daily train ride to and from Brno was the worst, because it took up time I truly did not have and the train was usually so overfilled I had no way to take advantage of the time to study. Occasionally, when the train was empty, I found a lone German soldier sleeping and would steal his revolver. One day, in an empty compartment, I saw a soldier removing his revolver and a belt full of ammunition and placing it on a shelf. I stole it, left the train at the nearest station, and walked the rest of the way to my bunker. Such opportunities could never be lost; acquiring weapons was very important for us, since we never could have enough of them.

Later that same evening we had some excitement at home. Uncle Joe suddenly showed up, opening the door without knocking and rushing in, sweating and out of breath.

"I'm on the run," he said urgently, "and this is the only place I can hide. It has become unsafe for me in my old hiding place above the Gestapo's office. They are looking everywhere for me."

As one of the resistance leaders, Uncle Joe was on the top of the wanted lists of both the SS and the Gestapo. He was constantly hiding or on the run so as not to blow his cover.

"Don't worry," my mother said. "We are all in this together."

She moved my sister from our shared bedroom to hers, and from then on my uncle and I bunked together. Our family established new rules about who could or could not come to our apartment. To make sure my uncle wouldn't be visible, we had to do everything for him. We made sure nobody from other apartments saw him going to the toilet; when he had to leave and then return, there was always someone with him; and I had to do more errands, especially in Brno, where he had several contacts. One of the main contacts that I kept for him was Captain Žárský, who was now a civilian and dealt in leather goods.

The days in school usually followed a routine, but sometimes events transpired that shook us to the core. In one instance, at 10:00 a.m., our math professor Dr. Syrový ordered us to open the windows that faced the Kaunitz College dormitory. Kaunitz was changed into a prison after Heydrich's assassination; now our patriots were locked up there, and on this day the guards were to execute someone by firing squad.

Our professor said to us, "Listen. Listen and never forget."

It would not be the last time he would utter those words. Differential equations seemed trivial then, as we realized the enormity and horror of the times.

About an hour later, the screams of the sirens announced an approaching air attack by the Allies. After it was over, we left the shelter and went out to the streets, where help was needed. A bomb had fallen a block from our school, so we ran there as quickly as we could. We heard cries and realized that children were trapped in the building's basement, which was flooding with water from broken pipes. We ran to the basement windows, but we could do nothing; an SS soldier was standing there with a rifle, and motioned for us to leave or risk being shot. We better comprehended this atrocity the next day, when we read the propaganda in the paper of how the Allies bombed little school children.

The ruthlessness of war made everyone callous and disheartened. Still, we started to receive news of the advancing Soviets, and after June 6, 1944, we heard about the invasion of Normandy, which later became known as D-Day. France was far away, however, and our own troubles continued.

In August we heard about an uprising in Paris and another a few days later in Slovakia; both uprisings were bloody and did not help much to liberate Europe. Our resistance leaders in Bohemia and Moravia did everything possible to keep our people calm, because powerful forces still among us could easily destroy any attempt against the Germans. However, by then it seemed inevitable that Germany would lose the war; the only question was when, and the major focus was to control people in occupied territories and keep them from attempting foolish rebellions in the face of the still dominant occupying troops. At the end of December the Soviet troops took Budapest. It was only a matter of time before they reached us.

In January of 1945, a few uninformed youth in our town began to talk about rising up against the Germans, and I mentioned this to my father and my uncle. Both were emphatic and explicit when they told me that they must be talked out of it, because the reprisals from the Germans would be costly. My father took it upon himself to set the young men straight for their own good and for the good of our community.

The behavior of the Germans grew ever more diverse and erratic. Many of them began to change their colors and became very friendly, while others were militant and ready to foment disorder just so they would have reasons for violence.

My school continued classes until the end of March, but we were instructed to come in only occasionally for assignments. My mother was concerned for my safety, but my father encouraged me to go; he felt I would be free from danger.

On the way home from school, I stopped one day with two friends at the barbershop in the neighboring village. The barber was cutting my hair when a large German military unit unexpectedly came marching by. The German soldiers always marched well, and it was a spectacle in a village where not much was going on. My two buddies had nothing else to do while I was getting my hair cut, so they stepped out of the shop to view the march. I could see them through the glass door; they were merely standing there and watching the lines of troops going by. Suddenly, a low-ranking SS officer broke formation, approached my friends as they stood at the barbershop door, pulled out his revolver, and shot them both in cold blood.

In an instant, the only two people who had befriended me or shown me any kindness were dead on the doorstep, an awful scarlet pool forming swiftly beneath them. The barber and I were petrified, thinking we were next in line to have our lives snuffed out; yet nothing happened. The soldier left and went back to the march, and I will never know why he did not turn on us.

In horror, I immediately headed toward home and told my father what had happened. He called a friend, and the three of us went out to trail the German company. We caught up with them at last, and discovered they were heading toward Znojmo on the Austrian border. I saw and identified the officer who had so mercilessly shot my friends, and pointed him out to my father's colleague. Father and I then returned home, and as we did, he told me his friend would take care of the bastard. While I experienced some satisfaction knowing this, I still felt my friends' loss keenly. I knew then, more than ever, that these were ugly times.

THE LONG RIFLE

The Wehrmacht was retreating from the Soviets, but as they did, they were also placing explosives to destroy anything the Russians could use.

On April 18, I observed from my bunker how a German demolition squad placed explosives within the structure of the nearby railroad bridge. The rail line was the only link between the capital city of Brno and the southern district of the Moravian province. The soldiers had come in a locomotive to place the charges and stretched the cables to a safe distance. I concluded that whoever would detonate the explosives would have to get there the same way. I also knew that no one else was aware of the Germans' activity. If the bridge were to be saved, it would be up to me.

The distance from my cave was about two hundred and fifty yards. None of my own weapons could reach that point accurately, and I knew I only had one shot. If I missed, the chance to save the bridge would be greatly diminished, and I myself would risk discovery.

I needed a long rifle to prevent anyone from reaching the end of the wires and completing the detonation. Only the Germans themselves had such rifles.

On the plain behind the cliff where my bunker lay were hundreds of tanks and trucks; they were the Sixth Panzer Division coming back from Stalingrad, and they had just arrived in our area. At my family's house the local street narrowed and ended, and then changed into a field trail. Dozens of the trucks lined this street, and I noticed that one of the types of rifles I needed was strapped on the inside of the driver's door of the last field truck. The truck with the rifle was the closest to the foot of the hill near my bunker in the cliff, but it was also very close to our house.

To prevent discovery, the long rifle had to be stolen at the last possible moment, before the Germans departed. If they found out about the missing rifle, many would suffer for it. There was no room for mistakes. My cue to get the rifle would be the start-up commotion of all the tanks; the departure of this formidable force would be preceded by the considerable disorder of the soldiers and general turmoil. The land would tremble from the vibrating engines.

I slept with my eyes half open.

In my cave and at home at night, I thought of the devastating consequences to my nation if the bridge were destroyed. After all the conflicts, the impoverished state would not be able to rebuild a rail line for a long time, and without it, lack of communication and industrial exchange would mean more hunger in the large cities and no products or supplies in the south. That bridge was as essential for us as air.

On April 21, 1945, long before dawn, the commander of the retreating Panzer Division received word about Berlin being surrounded by the Soviets; I myself heard it on the news from London. There was no other way out for the Germans. They were afraid to surrender to the Russians because of the devastation they had left behind in the Soviet territory; the division had to leave quickly to reach the American Zone safely.

The roar of the tanks filled the night as they prepared to depart, and on the streets, the number of guards doubled.

I sneaked out into the dark and cautiously waited for the patrol to pass to the other end of the street. Then I climbed into the driver's seat of the empty field truck to untie the rifle. The straps were dry and hard, and it took me longer to free the rifle and the ammunition than I anticipated. By then, the two patrolmen were returning from the far end of the street.

The beating of my heart seemed louder than the roar of the tanks as the guards almost touched the door when they passed by me. At the foot of the ridge, about two hundred feet from the truck, they turned back.

I held my breath once more, but I could not control my heartbeat; in the tight space between the seat and the pedals I almost choked from its pounding. My throat and mouth burned and my sweaty hands trembled with fright.

After a few moments, I peeked out to see the guards fading in the darkness. Quietly I unlocked the door and slid off the seat. At that moment, in the second floor window of the house where I lived, appeared the horrified face of my mother. I saw her silhouette there; her frightened form tight against the glass seemed to reflect a saintly image. She recognized me and saw what I did.

I had been hiding my activities from her for security reasons. Most of the time, however, she knew what was going on, and her strong convictions to fight for freedom silently reinforced our family's ideals. It was really not necessary to shelter her; yet I felt a searing pang of guilt when I saw her terror. She was still my mother.

I shut the truck door silently and swiftly vanished toward the dark hill with the rifle and ammunition.

When I got to the cave I relaxed, prepared the weapon, and hoped for daybreak so I could see. I knew the locomotive would come; I just did not know when.

In the morning light, that image of my mother in the window faded slowly from my mind as I realized what I was facing. I swallowed many times to moisten my throat, which seemed to grow drier with each passing second. I started to hope the locomotive would not come, that perhaps they had changed their minds or even forgotten.

Then, suddenly, it arrived. In a few seconds the steam brake stopped the locomotive. A soldier stepped down with a battery box in his hands and walked toward the cables.

He was going to blow up the bridge.

I had just one chance. I would not have another. After the first shot the soldier would be able to take cover and detonate the charges.

The long rifle was ready. I got the soldier in my sights as he was kneeling over the box. I squeezed the trigger slowly and took my shot.

When the engineer saw his partner fall down dead, he took off with the steam hissing and the wheels of the locomotive wildly spinning.

Shortly thereafter I heard several explosions from the city; I discovered later it was a clothing and shoe warehouse, the food supply warehouse, and the grain depository.

I remained still. In a few hours the whole territory became silent.

The era of German control had ended.

Then the Soviets took over for the next forty-five years.

four

"SOVIET LIBERATION": A NEW WAY OF WAR

My father could not understand
the mid-century chaos
that spread discontent
and disregarded people's right to live in peace.
Silently I watched his torment
over the conditions in which we found ourselves
when the war ended.
Politicians had not—
and still have not—
learned enough from history to prevent wars
murder, starving, pain, destruction, persecution, slavery,
and the practice of domination.
The war didn't end.
Peace was just postponed.

M Y FATHER AND I became disturbed by how the end of the war evolved. After suffering untold hardships for almost seven years, we expected a joyful liberation. After all, the actual retreat of the Wehrmacht from our town was relatively calm, without any civilian casualties; this was in large part thanks to my father, who had convinced the young men not to rise up against the Germans and to merely wait for them to leave.

The behavior of the Soviet Army, our liberators, disgraced the whole Allied war effort to the point that Eastern Europeans began to hate the Soviets. Eastern Europe was delivered up to the tender mercies of the would-be Soviet paradise, and I directly observed the slow decay within our traditional democratic state. The freedom for which we had paid so dearly turned into a social scheme of unbound terror, and people already devastated by war faced further uncontrolled persecution. We felt the West had abandoned us again.

Soon we found out about the Yalta and Teheran agreements, in which the West donated all the Eastern European nations to Daddy Stalin. This unbelievable turn of events beset all the countries behind what would be called the "Iron Curtain," countries unable to understand why the American president gave away the most loyal nations. This incompetent diplomacy would backfire, costing the world more wars. The Iron Curtain now divided the continent, and the name "Cold War" entered the dictionaries of the world.

Before we could establish order in our Republic, the Soviets slowly crept in and took over all the vital organizations within the military and the government. They filled the leading positions in private industries, businesses, and the offices of local communities, together with bumbling Czech collaborators. These newly enthusiastic Communists began to act alarmingly like the Gestapo and the SS, save for the fact that the Germans were more intelligent.

We had no choice. We continued our revolutionary activities, forming a new resistance. This time, however, it was harder, for we faced our own Czech neighbors, who had now become our enemies.

COLD WAR: 1945-1948

On April 28, 1945, just a few days after the German forces left our town, the Russian Armada moved in on the main highway leading from the Moravian capital of Brno, passing just a mile from our house. My father and I anxiously hurried to welcome the victorious army. At first, three or four two-wheeled buggies with soldiers pulled in; that was the whole "armada," and we did not see anything else for several hours. We thought that perhaps the strategy of the Russian forces was to show as little force as possible, and to hide their strength in the rear. Later, more soldiers appeared on the highway, but we could not ascertain how they had gotten there; we just assumed they walked in from the fields. We again tried to convince ourselves this slow approach was a trick, and that many more would soon come.

More did come—four field trucks full of additional troops—but so did very disturbing news. As they advanced, the Russian soldiers were robbing homes and raping women. We did not want to believe that such tales were true, but soon it became all too clear that they were; the victorious troops were violating the innocent and stealing objects to send home to Russia. Those who knew Russia and its socioeconomic conditions explained that many ordinary Russians never saw things that in our households were common, and because of this the Soviets considered us *burzhui*—bourgeois. They thought us rich, though the truth was far different.

So there it was. We were freed from one horror and plunged into another.

Earlier, we buried our firearms and ammunition deep in a deserted forest, safe in a waterproof container; we had hoped we would not have to use them again. Now we dug them out, in the event that we would have to defend ourselves anew.

These prospects began to darken our victory over Nazism. The Allies were more than a hundred miles to the west, so hope for the freedom we had imagined as we fought the Nazis faded.

In a few days, we noticed that the London newscasts had moderated their patriotic talks to us. Our new administration was overrun with Communists, and we, who had fought to save our country in the resistance, were forced to surrender our rights to the Communist Party of Czechoslovakia, which was directed by the Soviets. Many of these party members were former Nazi collaborators, and it made us angry to see how quickly they changed their colors. The Communists overpowered the Czech Intelligence Agency and the army. The Soviet Union and the NKVD, the All-Union Commissariat of Internal Affairs, became the ruling power of the liberated Czechoslovakia; before 1934, the NKVD had been the political police administration OGPU, and later in 1954 it became the KGB. The Stalinist "Great Purge" of 1934-1939 in the Soviet Union began to affect post-World War II Czechoslovakia as soon as she was freed and then reoccupied.

In June of 1945, I completed my second year of mechanical engineering study in Brno. Much time had been lost during 1944-45 because of the war, and I had to make up for it between semesters and during the following two years. I had no time for anything else; I was up to my neck in studies, but somehow I managed.

My Uncle Joe asked me to move into his sister's household in northern Brno, to help her son Jiři with math and to try to influence him to study regularly. He was about my age, attended the gymnasium, and was virtually addicted to music. He was a clarinet virtuoso, but the problem was that neither the gymnasium nor the music academies allowed him to play the instrument. He was also required to pass all academic subjects, in which he was failing.

I did not succeed in helping him with math and convincing him to study, because I also loved music. He held a job as a lead clarinetist in the Oasa Cabaret, which was located on the main street across from Lužánky Park. With his position in the band he arranged for a job as a singer for me; I could not refuse. For one evening program I made more money than what my father could give me for a whole month, and I enjoyed it immensely. Hence, Jiři's math went to hell, and I became a cabaret crooner. My own studies, however, I kept up with; I could not risk failure, for I did not dare disappoint my father.

November brought about nostalgic feelings for bygone days. The leaves were almost gone, and I found myself compelled to go to Náměšt to walk my hills. My thoughts raced through my head, swirling like the last leaves in the wind; I had brought my journal along, and stopped for a moment to record all that moved in my mind:

I walk slowly over a low ridge and muse over the intermittent murmur of a stream now cresting over its banks in the valley. Anxiously my eyes try to penetrate the fine bluish vapor emanating from the forests scattered around me and from the hills on the other side of the valley. I turn reluctantly from the colorful background to keep walking.

My gaze falls on parched grass stalks bordering my walk, now muddy after a gentle rain. Many water droplets wreathe the bent grass like small pearls, reflecting a stunning spectrum of crystal tears shattered by the toes of my shoes. I reach the top of the hill and suddenly a precious vision is revealed to me: the sun's rays reflecting red on the roofs of Náměšt. In the square is a church, a monument of old Gothic architecture; its bell chimes, imploring heaven, calling folk to pray. My sight moves from the church, over the statues on the stone bridge, and stops at the majestic castle. Its silhouette shines brightly from the blue-gray behind it. The massive battlements crown the enormous walls, seeming to resonate a festive tune to the countryside, as if singing about long-gone medieval glory. Wherever I look, nature triumphantly responds.

Here I lived for seven years, through beautiful and bad times.

All of this reminds me of the Low Tatras region in Slovakia; that was also my home, where I spent my youngest years. It was lovely there, until the Nazis brutally divided our Republic, and I, together with my family, had to depart. Knowing that I was not going to an utterly foreign country, I knew that here, in the place where I now stand, I would find another home, and that Moravia would surely give me all that I need.

I was not disappointed, and hoping that soon we would be free, I lived my sad youth until that freedom came, when everyone breathed a sigh of relief and I believed that I could start a new and happy life.

Now I work with joy, and shall try to prove that I am a worthwhile member of the human race.

Shortly after I wrote these words, the joy to which I looked forward vanished, and we all started a new struggle for survival.

After my communion with the countryside, I returned to Brno, refreshed, to continue my studies and my performances at the Oasa Cabaret. This continued through 1946, and up until the end of my third year of engineering.

One evening in June, my program was particularly pleasing for me as I sang medleys in several languages, accompanied by Jiři and the rest of the dedicated musicians. Suddenly, right at the table nearest to the stage, I saw one of my professors sipping wine. He almost choked on it as he lifted his head and saw me at the mic. Abruptly, he stood up, threw his money on the table, and ostentatiously walked out in a huff.

The next day in his class we had a showdown. He pointed his finger at me, shouting,

"You are a *whore*, mister, and you will never be an engineer! I will see you expelled from this institution!"

With that, he ran out, and in moments I was summoned to the dean's office, where I was told of the serious charges against me and that my father had been called to the school. I waited for him in the corridor; from all of my previous experiences, I knew he would want to speak with me first.

"Well, what have you done now?" he asked as he arrived.

After I explained what had happened, he said nothing and we entered the dean's office. The dean was rather calm, but the professor was extremely edgy.

Loudly, he demanded I be expelled, as it was undignified for a student of such an honorable institution to sing at such a nightclub.

In my defense, my father replied, "Might I ask what *you* were doing in that undignified club, then?"

That ended the whole argument.

I promised to stop singing at the Oasa as soon as a replacement could be found for me. My grade in that professor's course dropped to a C, and our relationship was never the same. Still, when I took the state exam in 1947, which was partially a verbal session before the state board that consisted of professors from several other engineering colleges, I passed. For that examination, and in addition to academic subjects, we obtained a pilot's license for a one-engine plane—something I had gained already in April of 1946—plus a driver's license for heavy trucks, and a license to operate heavy construction equipment.

After graduation, I started working as a draftsman at the First Brno Factory in the steam boiler department, but as soon as I matriculated in the law school at Masaryk University I quit that job. I detested the conditions and the socialistic atmosphere created by the newly appointed directors.

By then, the Czech Communists, aided by the Soviets, had spread their influence through all segments of government, manufacturing plants, and farming. All learning institutions yielded to the new Soviet order; entertainment and the arts were geared to proletarian ideals, and the former Czech traditions were abandoned.

I wondered how long my father would last in the police commissioner's position. Thus far, the Communists considered him politically friendly, as he had been in the Czech Legion in Russia during World War I; they were ignorant of the fact that the Czech Legion was the first organized military force fighting them in 1917. Uncle Joe had already been kicked around in his command; officers of much lower rank, being members of the Communist Party, were slowly taking over. He told me that soon we would all be kicked out. My sister held a high secretarial position in the state department; she was told to become a party member or experience consequences. My father also began to notice hostilities from higher-ups. Once again the clouds of a new war hovered darkly over us.

Before I could enter the law school, I was required to pass a special exam in Latin, which had not been part of the engineering school curriculum. The requirement was typical, and dated back to the Middle Ages; given the use of Latin terms in law, it was necessary to have a basic working knowledge of the language. Luckily, the engineering school's professor of the Czech language was fluent in classical Latin, and tutored me since the previous year; thus, I was prepared, and passed with relative ease.

Now law school demanded that I switch gears from my old method of study to a new one. I dove into it, eagerly searching the rich libraries to complete my assignments and spending most of my waking moments at the university; my studies there continued until June 2, 1948, my father's birthday.

In June of 1947, shortly after I quit the First Brno Factory job, I was told my uncle Joe needed me to travel to Zanzibar in Tanzania. I was to pick up some costly gems earmarked to finance the new resistance he was organizing with colleagues and friends, which was to be on the same scale as the one waged against the Germans. The help from Africa was not unexpected; my uncle had forged close ties with the Israelis during wartime. These alliances became more meaningful since the partitioning of nations after World War II affected the Czechoslovakians and Israelis equally. The Czechs worked hard to deliver intelligence from behind the Iron Curtain, furnished men trained in war strategy, and used political influence with the British to help form the new state of Israel. The Israelis possessed considerable wealth in southern African regions and had connections to transfer it to Central Europe; still, we had to go and retrieve it.

The Israeli commander suggested that the resistance dispatch an inconspicuous young and healthy lad, one who could withstand long distances and treacherous travel through hot deserts and cold mountains. Although my destination was Central Africa, the Israelis had a chain of reliable agents stationed in strategic locations all the way to the South African Republic, available to guide such a messenger safely through unfamiliar territories.

I had to memorize my itinerary and meet my guides at specified places; it was crucial I be on time and that I recognize them quickly and completely. My clothing was put together so I could change easily when

I reached southern Spain and crossed at Gibraltar. I was not to be concerned about food and money; the guides would aid me with everything. In case of the unexpected, my uncle gave me a few British pounds and shillings.

It took me less than a day to reach Tangier. Bypassing the Atlas Mountains through Algeria to the border of Niger, however, was more time-consuming. Between the mountains and traveling on an occasional decade-old, four-wheel drive, and intermittently joining a small group of contraband traders on camels, took three very sickening days. I grew nauseated from the unaccustomed motion and stench of animals. My guide, a middle-aged and very knowledgeable Brit, gave me some dry fruit that tasted like dried prunes, which eased my vomiting a bit.

From Algeria, around the Ahaggar Mountains, through Niger, Chad, and the southern Sudan, I was in the care of an Israeli agent who utilized a small aircraft, and we arrived at Burundi, east of the Congo Republic, in less than three days. From there I had a fascinating view of Mount Kilimanjaro.

The next day in Zanzibar, my guide introduced me to an Israeli agent from Madagascar, and before I was dispatched back with the same guide, I had at long last a pleasant bath, European food, and a good night's sleep.

In the morning I met with a man dressed in a white lab coat, who bade me to undress; thereafter I realized that I was to hide the jewels in a rather personal place. He fastened a soft leather pouch containing many diamonds under my scrotum and muttered in German, "Hopefully you will be able to tolerate it."

After a breakfast that was almost good enough to distract me from my discomfort, we went back to Burundi again, crossed the Congo River at Port-Empain in the Congo Republic, and then flew to Fort Crampel in the Central African Republic, with many stops to refuel and change pilots. During the night I tried to sleep, for the guide advised me to relax so that I would be ready for the hard trip to come.

We deplaned near Crampel and drove a short distance to join a small contraband expedition with a destination west of the Ahaggar Mountains. I found myself horribly ill again as I spent a week's worth of fifteen-hour days hanging onto a swinging camel.

When we finally arrived, I saw a small village of tents and a narrow coldwater stream from the mountains. I was exhausted, but my guide gave me a mere half-hour to rest before we took off in four-wheel drive vehicles into the desert of Algeria, heading toward Beni Abbés. I felt horrible, and stopped counting the days and nights.

In Beni Abbés the Israeli agent introduced me to my new British guide; I did not speak a word of English, and his German was just as bad. From Beni Abbés we made a short trip on mules with five other travelers, through a pass in the Atlas Mountains. It took us two days to get to Marrakesh, where my guide talked to a Spanish-speaking man who arranged for a flight to Gibraltar for us. Another British agent was waiting for us as we deplaned. He spoke broken Polish, which I understood; I thus enjoyed my time with him until we reached Milan, where an Austrian Czech took over and guided me to Vienna, a place in which I already felt at home.

Once back in Brno, my uncle's friend, a doctor, removed the valuable pouch from where it had been uncomfortably lodged. Several men eagerly came and began to measure the diamonds; one of the men proclaimed them magnificent, and from his suitcase took out many packs of bank notes for my uncle. I had completed my mission well.

This was one of the many times I helped Uncle Joe; yet such adventures were soon to come to an end.

UNCLE JOE CAUTIONS ME

One day my sister Vlasta told me to meet my uncle at the open air vegetable market in Brno; he wanted to see me. He had instructed her to tell me that I should meet him at the pharmacy at 1:00 p.m. A few days before, our government sent him to Russia as the military attaché representing the new Czechoslovakia, and I wondered what had happened. My sister already knew, but she wanted my uncle to tell me.

I had just finished my first year of law school, including all of the associated exams, and I felt like celebrating; however, this meeting, clouded with secrecy, made me apprehensive. I knew that 1:00 p.m. was precisely the time at which he would be passing by the pharmacy at the corner. From a distance, and at exactly 1:00 p.m., I watched him to see if he would give the sign, known only to us, that would tell me I should approach him. He did not give it, but kept on walking between two buildings around the corner into an alley, crossing his thumb and forefinger—a sign that I should meet him at the crosswalk, out of sight of the market. This meant he was being watched from the marketplace. I crossed around the old buildings, and when I was out of view from the open plaza I ran to the end of the walk, where he had entered through a large wooden gate into a decrepit covered drive. By then I was at his side and walked with him into a garden surrounded by an old stone wall. There we sat, and after a short pause he told me what had happened and what needed to be done.

Uncle Joe had always treated me as an adult, even when I was as young as eleven. Since the last time I talked to him, his face had changed. It had aged, and today I read fear in it. At that moment, I felt as I had in Slovakia ten years before, when the Germans took over my country. Uncle's manner was very grave, and I could detect uncommon emotion in his eyes; he was on the verge of tears. He looked like my father had in 1939, when he told me he was wrong about my never needing to go and fight in a war.

My uncle told me that he never made it to his position in Moscow as envoy; instead, he had been arrested in Lvov and sent back to Czechoslovakia in chains, where he found himself under a new officer directed by an NKVD agent from the Soviet Union. He had been demoted, stripped of all his rights as an officer of the general staff, and released into civilian status. He knew they were following him, expecting he would lead them to others in the resistance.

If the secret service saw me talking to him, I would be followed and eventually arrested. He told me he had risked seeing me to arrange for my way out; I must go to Prague and join a Professor Kominek, who was already waiting for me. He wanted me to work for Kominek as I had done for my uncle himself. The necessary paperwork at Masaryk University in Brno had been taken care of and provided me student status at Charles University in Prague, and also a student job at the Ministry of the Interior. I would have to ask my family, friends, and others who knew me to say I was in Slovakia or somewhere else in the country. I should stay with Kominek as long as I could and if I ever lost my cover, I should leave the country, change my name, change my nationality, and establish a new life somewhere else, forgetting all about the old world.

He warned me to be on a sharp lookout for shorter men from the east, those with close-set eyes and rounded noses, well-built forms, and great, strong fists. There were many men like this in the country already, and they were the agents of the NKVD—soon to be the KGB. I had better fear them, for they were the best, and they were cruel.

He told me he doubted we would ever see one another again.

All of this sounded horribly ominous, and I was terrified.

My uncle then hugged me, the first time he had ever done so, and said how much he respected and loved me.

After our talk, my uncle returned to the market so the two men who were trailing him could pick up his track again; in this way, I could observe them from the other side of the square and learn how to identify them.

My uncle's form was soon lost amidst the crowds and the streets. It was the last time I ever saw him.

ESCAPE TO PRAGUE

After seeing my uncle, I went directly home, gathered all of my belongings, and packed a small bag. Then I went to the post office with many postcards, which were addressed to Vlasta, Jiři, and another friend from the Symphony Orchestra of Brno, in which I played violin. I dated the cards progressively in my own hand, and mailed them to Etelka, asking her to put the cards in the mailbox with corresponding dates so they would arrive in Brno as if I had sent them from Slovakia. This would buy me time to avoid the state police while in Bohemia.

From the post office I went to our contact at Masaryk University, who already had prepared papers with my new alias. I was to be Karel Zpívák of Husovice, Brno, a student at Masaryk University, who was finishing his first year; I would enter Charles University's history department and live in Malá Strana, Prague.

In those days, there was no fingerprinting for identification purposes, and I was safe for the moment as I entered my second-floor, one-room apartment in Malá Strana. Professor Kominek had arranged the rent with an elderly widow. The room was simply furnished, with enough space for my books, notes, and extensive maps of Prague, which I studied very carefully. I had two exits in case of an emergency: one was the window, which faced the maze of passages between old buildings, intricate rooftops, and side streets; the other, from a small corridor, led to a narrow medieval street overcrowded by vendors and parked vehicles. It took me several days to get acquainted with this labyrinth.

From my apartment, the network of political organizations and offices was just twenty minutes away. I was assigned to the Ministry of the Interior to collect data about the movement of agents, to discover plans for arresting citizens, and to learn how the Communist Party would overpower the government. I had my hands full, because all of this required that I proceed very cautiously as a young student of history who wanted to learn how to be useful to the socialist regime. I had a good chance of success approaching my job in this way; there were employees who liked to speak about their work, and often good information came my way. I was a good listener, and soon the young generation of various departments, appointed to execute tasks for their seniors, became my best informers without realizing it.

During my first days, Prague introduced me to a world of medieval treasures, carefully assembled and crafted as if just for me and as I had always imagined them. Charles IV had planted them in the city many centuries before to illuminate nations with the splendor of the arts. In a better era, they would have been enough to sustain me with their magic and beauty, but they were not why I was there. I was caught in insensitive times that disdained such things.

My exposure to authorities in Brno had been minimal, and in Prague I was virtually unknown. My job there was not difficult, but it could get risky; I had to be alert day and night. It was exciting to get an assignment that required expertise in dealing with the enemy in high places. I thought and hoped it might be easier than what I had to do with the German language during the war. The results would be far-reaching if I succeeded; our underground would have a chance to join forces with the Hungarian and Polish movements against the Soviets.

The resistance organizations in all the countries behind the Iron Curtain were weak because they were not unified, and were thus vulnerable and facing overwhelming odds. Therefore, we thought that with good intelligence deliveries to the Americans, we would gain attention; the Americans would be an excellent unifying force and would help us shake the Soviets.

The Czechoslovakian underground was in constant danger. Since World War II, many patriots had changed over, and one could never tell who might be a traitor. On the surface, the communist doctrine was seductive to many who had the proletarian tendency; vulnerable to being recruited by the Communist Party, these Czechs formed a risky bunch because we could not identify which side they were on. In larger cities such cases seemed to reproduce, and for us the best thing was to appear ignorant, as if we knew nothing.

In truth, I myself knew too much, though I dearly wished that I did not.

ARREST IN PRAGUE

The air was oppressive on that July afternoon in Wenceslas Square. I was in a crowd of office workers congregating on the sidewalks during the noon break. Dressed in light trousers and a button-down shirt, I dangled a fashionable briefcase. Such briefcases were the trademarks of students and office workers, and I had to look just like all the others; it was crucial that I blend into the typical cityscape.

At this point in 1948, Prague was in pain. Past events, when the whole nation was brought to its knees, still overwhelmed the city.

Wenceslas Square, the entire city, and the country were in despair. On this day, it was obvious not much had changed since the close of the war—perhaps just the enemy. Flags with swastikas had been exchanged for flags with red stars, sickles and hammers.

I tried to remain calm as I noticed out of the corner of my eye that a policeman was approaching me.

"May I see your identification?" he asked tersely.

I turned to him and said, as I reached for my student I.D., "Of course, here it is."

"You are not a Praguer," he mumbled, scanning my I.D. booklet. "Your accent escapes me, though. Hmm . . . ah, I see. You are a Brüner."

"Yes," I answered confidently, though inside I grew more nervous, as it occurred to me that this unnecessary exposure to authority could mean trouble now that I was an official member of the resistance. My best bet was to be polite and to cooperate, and to hope my cover would hold up.

"Well, we're jumpy, aren't we?" the policeman insinuated. "And what might we be doing here in Prague, eh?"

I was not jumpy at all, but police officials always tried to make their victims tense by hinting that they were showing guilt; this made it convenient for them to pretend suspicion, a reason good enough for arrest.

"I am studying history," I replied in a calm, even tone.

"Why are you so nervous?" he asked with a singsong, sarcastic voice. "After all, I don't bite."

In those days people were seized for any reason, just to fill the arrest quota of a policeman. This one was a busybody, someone who enjoyed such work; by midday, he probably already had a long list of arrests.

"Well, well . . . Something is just not quite right about you," he said, pulling out a notebook from his breast pocket and writing in his eleventh arrest: me. "We better check you out."

He spitefully led me to the station on the second floor of a building that stood just around the corner. After a short interrogation, I was released; they had nothing on me and, therefore, could not hold me.

As I walked down a flight of stairs, an inspector who was coming up recognized me as he passed; he had seen me frequently in the building of the Ministry of the Interior. Inspector Janoušek correctly assumed I was a ministry employee and engaged me in casual conversation; I was trapped, unable to shake him. Unfortunately for me, his suspicion of me grew, as he found me out of place. Before I could leave, he forced me into his office, where he himself began to interrogate me.

The questioning escalated and lasted through the night. Janoušek, being under pressure from superiors and eager to better himself in the new People's Republic, made an unusual and protracted effort to get more out of me; he hoped to break a case that would get him recognition and a reward. He thought he was face-to-face with someone who might have a clue to a certain "big case" everyone on the force was after; if he could obtain the clue, then he would finally be in the spotlight and might even get some honors from the Party. He bit his lip and slowly pulled gloves over his sweaty hands.

I knew someday this might happen, and I was prepared for it. I knew that work in the resistance offered no shelter or safety for anyone; however, I always imagined that if anything were to go wrong, it would be in action, with guns popping. My arrest was a farce; I had been picked at random during my lunch break, at which time I had been far from anything that resembled a rebel. I was taken when I was daydreaming, arrested for nothing.

Janoušek's fists worked me over. At first it hurt terribly; later, I became numb. I clenched my teeth and hoped I would remember this man well, so I could return the favor someday. I wondered how in the hell I had gotten myself into the situation.

Though I wished I would never have to, I now had a chance to use all the training to resist pain, hunger, threats, and torture that I had learned since 1939 from resistance agents and my father and uncle.

I was in a great deal of pain from the punches, which came fast and furious. Recollecting memories helped distract me from the intense reactions of my senses.

I am a strong twenty-year-old, born in Slovakia near the Hungarian border. My father is a Czech police officer, my mother is Hungarian . . .

I kept my mind ever busy.

They run a strict, patriotic Czech household. I have been studying law since 1947. This is supposed to be my first summer break after a heavy load of subjects that, for an engineer, were challenging and strange. . .

Less than five weeks before, my uncle had instructed me to leave Brno and to join Professor Kominek in Prague, and I immediately followed the order. How could I have been caught so soon, and in such a silly circumstance? I needed to withstand the beating, so I forced my thoughts to return inward, to entertain myself in spite of the pain; I went on remembering.

Heydrich's assassination, the destruction of Lidice, the end of the war . . . My short but happy time with the symphony orchestra in Brno . . . The February Prague uprising this year against the Communists had excited all of us . . . My experiences made me a much-needed revolutionary . . . That uprising had failed, but to resist was the only thing we could do . . .

Janoušek's fists seemed to beat these issues out of my brain while the pain faded on and off in my body. The guard wiped my face with a wet towel as Janoušek left, exhausted.

In came a lawyer, supposedly appointed for my defense but really just a puppet planted to make me talk. They made it easy for me not to say anything, for their questions did not even fit my case. Not once did they ask anything that could even remotely identify my guilt. They did not even know my real name, and they did not know any specific plot in which I might fit; Janoušek only knew that I had been seen many times in the Ministry of the Interior's building. He was merely speculating; I was guilty all right, but he did not know of what.

The beating began anew, and I retreated again to my thoughts and memories.

Since June I have lived in the Small Side Quarter, a historical subdivision of Prague, which retains its traditional architecture. On my desk and on a small night table close to my bed, I have several history and art books that I study in my spare time. Several maps, indicating the locations of significant monuments, almost cover an old drawing stand where I pore over the intricate layout of the city.

I was grateful that my thoughts protected me from the overzealous interrogator's punches. Despite his rising anger, his blows seemed to become less painful over time, and my resistance grew. I kept holding onto all that floated through my mind, letting him beat me as long as he liked, hoping he would not create permanent damage.

After World War II, Uncle Joe began to hint that my future should be in politics and told me that Brno had one of the best law schools in the country, perhaps in the world. His wife, my Aunt Helena, had dreams of me being the president of our country one day. My uncle took me to a law school graduation, introduced me to several lawyer friends, and I knew the direction I was expected to take.

My interrogator became tired. When he stopped yelling and hitting me, my pain increased. My neck vertebrae were stiff; I could not turn my head. I prayed it was temporary, and returned to my memories.

I joined Pavel Kominek in June, after I finished my first year of law school. A professor of biology at Charles University, he was denounced as an enemy of the state earlier in the year. Minutes before he was due to be arrested by the Communists, he disappeared and joined the ranks of patriots already hiding in the woods and mountains; soon he became their leader, a figure of hope. He admired my undying patriotism and experience from the Nazi years; I didn't know it when we first met, but he knew my background well and had special plans for me in his program to unite all the resistance movements against the Soviets. I became one of his most trusted helpers, and aided him in making new contacts and planning strategies. Disguised, he moved freely throughout the country, evading capture. What would happen to him now that I had been arrested? I hoped he would find someone else to fill my slot.

Drowsy in the bloodstained chair, I resolved to stay alert. The blood from my mouth dried on my chin; I felt how it seemed to shrink the skin, tightening it, and began to peel off when I moved my jaw. Frightened as I was, I still forced myself, by some inner strength of will, to hold on.

At great risk we collected intelligence about the Czech and Soviet communist activities and delivered it to United States forces in Bavaria, hoping for their support in fighting the enemy. I am dedicated to Pavel's work and proud of him. I am convinced that our work is noble and

that we are fighting the good fight, but I did not expect my arrest. What
should I do? What would my father have done?

The dark night fell, and finally I was left alone.

In the morning Janoušek returned refreshed, and once again I was
beaten into oblivion. After the pummeling I stared silently at the angry
policemen through two terribly swollen eyes; I could scarcely see their
faces through the slits. Then, suddenly, my stomach heaved, and I heavily vomited up all of the food that the guard had given me earlier.

"Nothing!" Janoušek hissed, furious. "This bastard is either innocent or stupid. We better let the specialists handle him."

"We've got to get something out of him, though, to have a reason
to send him there," said the man behind me. He jerked off his bloody
gloves. "Maybe he's too far gone. We'd better slow down."

Janoušek pulled open my eyelid to check. "We'll turn him over to
Pankrác, the central prison, and let them take responsibility. Write up a
transfer while I wash him up a little."

I grasped the motive for his concern, because the only evidence
against me was the mere suspicion that I was an enemy agent; now
he trembled from both exhaustion and the doubt that suddenly overwhelmed him. With a wet cloth, he wiped my face quickly and offered
me a drink of water. I moaned, and as the straps were removed, my arms
fell alongside the wooden chair. My body sank, my head lolled back,
and I wanted to scream, but I did not allow myself to do so. I could not
stop myself from asking, "Why me?"

I lost all of my courage, and a gurgle in my throat disgorged more
blood from my mouth. For me, this revolution had ended. "How
strange," I thought, "that for me it will end here in Prague."

I did not know that it was really just the beginning.

My body alternated between numbness and agony. I attempted to move, lifting my right hand over the chair arm, but it slipped over the sticky blood. I slouched, utterly depleted, and tried to center myself. I did not have a chance, for I heard a policeman reporting to Janoušek that they had searched my room but found nothing.

My face twitched as, in a half faint, I heard the guards mentioning the name of a prison; yet I could not make it out. Pavel had told me that in some of these dungeons, prisoners were tortured with the same medieval weapons used during the Inquisition. The prospect of being thrown into one of these awful places petrified me, but a punch and another round of senseless questioning from Janoušek brought me back to the present.

"What are you doing in Prague?" he demanded. "If you study in Brno, why aren't you there? What are you doing snooping around in the government buildings here? What were you doing in Wenceslas Square? Who do you work for?"

This approach would never work for him, but he did not know any better, it seemed.

Finally, I was transferred to the Pankrác State Prison, where Inspector Janoušek received some encouragement and continued his brutal treatment of me. Obsessed with the hope of advancing his position, he kept up with his interrogation, now under the supervision of an unnamed specialist.

Days went by; exhausted, we both stubbornly persisted. My training in how to resist pain gave me the strength to hold on despite losing consciousness from time to time; Janoušek was afraid to stop and afraid he would lose face before his peers. My anger toward him grew, hardening my resolve.

He struck me once more in the face, screaming, "Who is your contact? What are you doing in Prague?"

The blood on my face flowed and dried many times over; the stench of my unwashed body mixed with the smell of blood. I dozed off frequently, so they splashed my face with ice-cold water to keep me awake. Finally, two uniformed guards dragged me to the loading dock and shoved me into a van, slamming the steel door behind me.

The van felt like an oven. As it started to move, I heard words like "high treason" and "crimes against the people," but at that point I was too physically exhausted to be fully aware of what was going on or what the consequences would be. I lay on the metal floor of the van, which had been cooked by the blazing July sun. The bumps and jolts of the vehicle as it traveled knocked out the last of my senses.

In Prague, none of the officials had the guts to accept responsibility for my case, so I was transferred to another nameless prison. It was an old fortress that had fallen into disrepair. Faintly, I watched myself, almost as if from afar, being driven to one of the medieval ruins where the torture of inmates entertained some of the mentally disturbed jailers.

At the destination, the van backed up to a stone platform. Two men pulled me out, letting me fall on the cobblestones, and a pail of water was poured over me to encourage me to walk on my own; I was unable to do so. I was dragged to a small cell with a porthole just below the ceiling.

After the hot ride in the van, the cold and humid stone floor and walls felt pleasant. The heavy wood door, bound with rusty steel bands, had an opening at the top, but it was impossible to see out; it was too high. The cell was dark; the porthole let in only weak daylight, which faded even more in the deep space. The smell of urine and a dirty bucket for excrement filled the foul, damp, and barely ventilated cell; moisture was condensing on the walls and dripping. Somehow, I fell asleep despite a pulsating pain, barely able to remember the events of the day before.

The sound of a far-off church bell woke me into grim reality. It was pitch black in the cell, and I had to orient myself by feeling for the door. Opposite of it had to be the outside wall with the porthole.

Then the cover of the door hole opened, and the jailer handed me a bent aluminum cup filled with water. I sipped it slowly; my tongue was crushed, and I could not swallow without burning pain. I sat on the floor, leaning against the door, as I listened to the ringing bell and imagined the fields shadowed after sunset. Farmers would be returning home after a long day's work, walking and riding the field wagons laden with tools and harvest. Though they may not have realized it, they were the lucky people; thinking that I was working and suffering for their happiness almost made me smile a little, as I fell asleep once again, unable to keep my eyes open.

The next day some strength returned, but the pain had increased, and I felt forlorn. Realizing that I was receiving only water, just once a day, I recalled hearing about the famous hunger torture Pavel had mentioned. It meant being deprived of food for three days, ingesting only water. Then one would be given a plate full of pork, dumplings, and sauerkraut.

Days later I stared at a plate loaded with my favorite food. My mouth ached and my jaws cramped in a sharply contracting spasm; I salivated, my gut twisted, and my hands trembled. The whole plate was mine; I could eat it. Yet I knew the pain it would produce within me if I did, so I just sucked a little on the dumplings and the bone and, later, just sipped some water. It was extraordinarily difficult to resist the temptation to eat; the jailer was not pleased that I managed to do so.

On Tuesday, I met with the master jailer in his office. He shoved me into a corner and ordered me to stare into a mirror placed in front of me. At my sides, facing the mirror, he put two high-intensity lamps. There I saw my face for the first time in many days. Blue, swollen, bloody features made me realize, in stark clarity, that all the beatings had been real.

I was not allowed to close my eyes; every time I did, I was beaten over my back and shoulders. Early in the afternoon I collapsed, unconscious.

Later on, in the cell, I heard again the evening bell from the village, and I counted my sixth day in the nameless hole. I couldn't figure out to which medieval ruin it belonged; I just assumed it was about one hundred kilometers north of Prague. It did not seem to be on my memory map at all.

I felt as if my eyes had been clawed out; I touched them carefully to make sure they were still there. A sharp burning in them prevented me from sleeping and, in the dark, I began to panic in a phobic terror, helpless.

I did not realize until the following morning that I had somehow been totally blinded.

As the guards dragged me through one of the chambers where before I had seen a large stretching wheel, I now saw nothing. In horror I screamed, "I can't see, you bastards! You made me blind! I can't see, you whores, I can't see!"

I started to weep, but the more I cried, the more my eyes hurt. The guards just laughed, enjoying the spectacle of my dismay.

The next interrogation was brief. Now that I was blind, the jailers had to move me around. They pushed me up to an elevated stretcher, tied my hands and legs, and ripped off my pants. Then I felt the excruciating and precise grip of cold metal pincers upon my testicles.

The interrogator said with a sneer, "*Now* do you want to talk?"

At that point, I was nigh ready to talk; but what was I to say? Again, the wrong questions were asked, and I could give them nothing except my screaming curses, "Oh, what the hell! Shit on you, you bastards!"

Merciful unconsciousness saved me from my agony.

Later on, when I came around in my cell, the pain was in my sides, close to my kidneys. The jailer brought some bread and water, placing the cup in my hand because I was unable to move.

I scarcely touched my privates, even when urinating; they were terribly sensitive and painful. The bastards had crushed them, which caused me to pass out.

That evening, I barely heard the bells, and I thought I might be close to my end.

My ears rang continuously from pressure within, as if blood had run up to my temples and back down to my kidneys in a never-ending cramp. When the pulsating spasm struck I wanted to die, but when it passed, even if only for a short while, I trembled from the fear of dying. The inability to see twisted my thoughts and I panicked. I could not sleep, for I had awful nightmares, and a fear of what was to come next tormented me. By the next morning I had lost all sense of time. I became delirious; yet it was a blessing in disguise, for in my delirium I became indifferent, and disengaged from stress and terror.

The torturer lost his lust for more screams as he ruptured my fingers with vise grips, and on the following day—a Friday, they said—I was told the tribunal had found me guilty of high treason, and I would be executed by a firing squad on Monday.

"They are doing me a favor," I thought, wondering why; firing squads were generally reserved for military personnel. I did not know that sixteen other men were to be executed as well, and that the use of the firing squad was a mere convenience.

In an ironic twist, I came to like my cell; in it, I was safe, and in it, I was still alive. I wanted to live, no matter how much it hurt.

In the morning of Sunday, July 25, I once more heard the early church bell, and I dreamt of a small village surrounded by misty fields and meadows. I imagined the fresh, moist earth as a maiden after her morning bath. The river, covered with light fog, seemed as if it were waiting to come out from the twisting tree-covered valley.

I thought it would be my last faint taste of some small, beautiful moment of life.

THE RESCUE

A rescue from a medieval ruin in northern Bohemia was not likely. The fortress where I was held was surrounded by high, massive walls and guarded by many; nearby a tank depot housed armed mechanics, providing additional protection for the prison. The closest town was five miles away.

Pavel Kominek had for some time analyzed the possibility of rescuing sixteen men already there, and also the chance of somehow damaging the prison in order to discourage the communist police from continuing to use it. Recently his undercover man working inside the prison told him that yet another man had arrived, and he was being severely beaten. This was not unusual in and of itself; anybody arrested was severely beaten. Still, Pavel knew who it must be. He hurried his plans so as not to come too late.

It would be a daring act to attempt to get seventeen men out, but when Pavel received word that they all—including me—were to be shot, he set up the rescue at once.

About a mile from the prison, the tank depot serviced trucks and tanks, and after repairing the equipment, the mechanics also test-drove it on large fields that stretched hundreds of acres between the depot and the prison. Pavel's plan was to hijack two tanks and a truck from the testing grounds and plow them through the prison walls, pick up the prisoners, and leave. Timing was imperative.

"I am desperate," Pavel told his companion Dr. Podlipný. "Some of my best men had disappeared and for a time, I didn't know where they were. Then one of my men in Pankrác heard about this ruin."

The Communists called these boys "hopeless," Pavel continued to explain, because they had been arrested without cause and were terribly mistreated during interrogation. "The unqualified personnel in the police force didn't know how to justify their arrests and beatings, sometimes killings. So, they concealed their own criminal actions by locking up the innocent, wiping away all traces of them.

"It has taken some planning," Pavel said, "but when I heard that more boys had been arrested, I knew I had to get them out! Tomorrow will be too late; they're to be shot at dawn. I have two slick agents in the fortress posing as devoted party members and employed as assistant jailers; at the given moment, they will disable the telephone and the sirens."

The next part of the plan was for Pavel to send four experts to place explosives under the fortress wall that faced the small bridge over the stream. Then the men would hide under that bridge through the night until the next day when it was time to detonate the explosives.

As Pavel, Podlipný, and the crew approached the testing field in a car, they did not see any tanks or trucks. Pavel reasoned that the vehicles were still in the shop. Immediately altering his plan, he told the driver to go around the small forest so as to approach the depot shop from behind.

The road leading from the proving grounds to the nearly deserted tank depot was rocky, and ended at a waste dump just a few feet from the corner of the garage. The car was not visible from the buildings.

In the shop, four mechanics on duty since 8:00 a.m. now lay in the shade of the greasy garage; other depot employees had gone to town for a holiday. The mechanics, assigned to test-drive equipment that Sunday, had been off duty the day before and had indulged in some routine drinking. For them, Sunday mornings, free of supervision, were a welcome relaxation, a chance to sleep off hangovers.

"I will enter first," Pavel whispered tersely. "No shooting! We are just a few minutes late and my plan will work best without noise and casualties. You all know what to do. Let's go!"

He was wearing an officer's uniform, and now masked his face with a scarf as he jumped off the passenger seat and calmly approached the large, open sliding door of the shop. The scarf over his face added to the element of surprise as he walked in. Sleepy men jumped up and saluted as he entered; then, halfway through their salutes, their hands froze on their foreheads and they grimaced as they saw the mask.

The astonished mechanics offered no resistance and clumsily obeyed Pavel's commands. Revolver in hand, he forced them into an office space at the back of the shop. Three other masked men, after checking the fuel content in the machines, quickly mounted two tanks and a combat truck. The man who had driven Pavel and his crew drove unseen to town by way of farm roads; his job ended for the moment, as he was to observe events in town and report to Pavel.

The fifth masked man, Dr. Podlipný, walked in behind the mechanics and injected each with a sleeping drug; he knew their bodies were practically saturated with alcohol and little was needed to put them to sleep.

"Well, they'll sleep all day," Pavel mumbled from under his mask as he locked the door behind them and jumped on the moving truck. The doctor followed, and the three vehicles rumbled about three kilometers across the testing field, directly toward the fortress that was barely visible on the eastern horizon. The dust behind the vehicles and the roaring engines made things appear as they always did during Sunday morning testing.

The two tanks stopped before reaching the bridge, while the field truck drove closer to the river where the driver could observe the predetermined slingshot signal in the water—a sign that the telephone and sirens inside the prison had been disabled.

Considering the delay caused by having to approach the depot shop from behind, everything went well. Even the men waiting under the bridge, having become worried and restless about a delay they didn't understand, held true.

When the tanks finally appeared at the far end of the bridge about one hundred meters from the wall, one man under the bridge synchronized himself with the speed of the tanks and, using a portable battery, made successive electric contacts to two strategically located explosives under the fortress wall.

The powerful charges cleared a path for the tanks to enter a large courtyard. The two explosions were not as noisy as one of the same power, and merged well with the usual activity that occurred during Sunday testing. From the bridge, the roaring machines—the two tanks first—drove quickly over the stone rubble in a cloud of dust and smoke, coming to a sudden stop at the archway of the guard office. The men under the bridge leaped up the embankment, climbed through the opening in the wall, and joined the others inside.

With automatic weapons they overpowered the drowsy jailers in seconds, without having to fire a shot. Pavel's two undercover men subdued the sentries on duty near the cells. As Pavel expected, the swift surrender of the guards resulted from the quick, unexpected entry.

When the cell doors opened, sixteen prisoners dragged themselves as fast as they could manage onto the truck; I was carried out on a stretcher, semiconscious. The guards were locked in cells unharmed; Pavel knew they would be punished enough later for allowing the break.

The tanks, after riding over the exploded wall once more to level the path, were disabled, and the truck carrying all of us sped away from the prison, storming eastward through the deserted fields. Dr. Podlipný sedated some of us with pain medication, wiped off the dried blood, and examined me for any visible broken bones. The burning sting from the disinfectant, which he applied to my open wounds, awakened me from my daze. Although I was still too incapacitated to fully understand what was happening, I realized I had been rescued; I was relieved beyond all telling, but I was still blind.

After bypassing the small village on the west bank of a river, the truck suddenly stopped. Everyone was transferred to waiting civilian vehicles, which dispersed in different directions. The armored truck was driven backward in its own tire marks for about two hundred meters, then turned west on a paved road and driven into heavy woods.

Pavel expected the authorities to notice the breakout at noon, when food from the village had to be delivered to the guards. Escapees had at least an hour head start to vanish into the countryside. Like a flock of birds they scattered, and in minutes all was silent.

My friends placed me in the back seat of their vehicle and we headed south. At my side, Dr. Podlipný dozed off, while Pavel slumped beside the driver Miloš and mused over his triumph. After stopping at a small town, they changed clothing and then swapped vehicles at two check-points. To avoid the National Safety Federation police, they traveled slowly, on side roads.

At about 5:00 p.m., as we approached the Šumava Mountains in southern Bohemia, the car turned onto a dirt road. The area must have been overgrown with pines since I heard branches scraping the car as we moved deeper between them; after some time, the car came to a halt. My friends had the kindness to describe the journey and the surroundings even now, so I would not panic in my continuing blindness.

Miloš walked back to the entry and used a branch to sweep away the tire prints; then he drove to a shabby log cabin where, helped by Pavel and Podlipný, he placed me on a layer of hay in the back of an already harnessed one-horse buggy. Pavel and Podlipný made themselves comfortable beside me, as Miloš drove the car into a narrow lean-to, removed the battery, and hid it in the cabin. He covered the car with branches and pulled the barn door shut; with a large branch he swept away the tracks, then hopped onto the carriage seat and jerked the horse toward the hills.

We reached Camp Šumava before 8:00 p.m. I was taken to a cabin where another doctor waited to attend to my eyes and broken fingers. After that, the whole camp became silent.

I grasped the magnitude of the day's actions as my friend and soon-to-be trainer, Vasil, spoke to me about the raid. In spite of my sedation, my awe at the scope of the occurrence kept me from falling asleep. I was incredibly proud of Pavel and the ideology of the resistance, and was honored to be a part of it, despite the cost.

Dr. Podlipný was also very helpful, attending to my wounds and telling me later what happened while I was unconscious.

The prison rescue astounded the communist government and provoked the Soviet secret police everywhere in Czechoslovakia to investigate the daring raid. The surprise rescue—with so few injuries and no deaths—caused embarrassed officials to order a total news blackout; the daily press mentioned nothing about the escape.

The following day, as the authorities originally planned, the newspapers listed the names of the seventeen condemned—my pseudonym among them—and announced that their execution for high treason had taken place at dawn on Monday, July 26. Their families did not know what had actually happened, and the resistance leaders, for everyone's protection, kept it secret for a long time.

My sister read the Monday paper, recognized my undercover name, and mourned my death; eventually she told my parents, and for them it was devastating.

Living in Czechoslovakia was now reduced to mere survival. All people became suspect, and even the purely innocent were arrested. My father lost his job; the communist authorities confiscated his property and his "friends" stopped calling. Before the year's end, the police arrested my sister, and in 1949 sentenced her to death for high treason.

Much later I learned her ultimate fate: Embarrassed by the harsh sentence on a woman, the Review Board of the Soviet Communist Party—including some Russian women's organizations, which then had strong influence in Czechoslovakian affairs—ordered a retrial, changing the sentence to eighteen years of hard labor. To avoid another rescue, the vexed authorities guarded Vlasta well, moving her from one prison to another. Word also reached me then of my Uncle Joe's arrest and trial in 1949, which I learned had produced another death sentence in the closed circle of my family.

Everywhere, Czechoslovakians were abandoning their homeland, fleeing from arrest, persecution, and death.

Camp Šumava sheltered about a hundred fugitives who needed temporary protection for a few days' stay before crossing the border into Bavaria. They were lucky to have gotten this far, persecuted as they were by the Communists. Some, simply because they opposed current political ideology, were in mortal danger in their own countries from their own countrymen. Many of them were the intellectuals or the economically better off, which the new government considered bourgeois and therefore a capitalistic, anti-Socialist element.

One job of the Czech underground movement was to help these runaways to get safely over the border. To cross the wild frontier territory illegally was treacherous, and many lost their lives to the communist border patrols and their dogs, or simply because the height of the cliffs overwhelmed them.

Camp Šumava was only accessible to a few who passed the screening of Pavel or his associates in the resistance; this screening was strict, so as to safeguard the secrecy of the camp. The lucky ones who were considered reliable enough to go "over the hills" were brought to the camp blindfolded, and were thus unable to reveal anything in the event they were caught. They would be instructed about the hike and what to do if captured by the border guards; our guides showed them the trail to the closest point where the crossing would be the safest. These people's stay was temporary, and they were kept separate from those of us who actively participated in the underground. Violation of our anonymity would lead to exposure and doom; therefore, we never mingled with strangers and remained secluded among our own ranks. We became withdrawn and lonely; even among ourselves we routinely avoided making friends, for to lose a friend in action was hard. Although our commitment to each other surpassed the most sincere brotherly loyalty, our training required that nothing interfere with our duty; the simplest error or lapse in judgment could have serious consequences, not just for individuals, but also for our entire organization.

With some more permanent features than the refugees' shelters, our housing had more comfortable beds, more privacy, and more storage space, but it was all easily dismantled and moved in case of an intrusion. This flexibility kept us ahead of various police, and we earned the reputation of not being easily apprehended. The mountains, cliffs, and impenetrable woods kept us safe, but the harsh elements lashed unmercifully at the desolate forest far from civilization. The hills offered only limited protection; our sentries constantly guarded the valley pass where an unwanted intruder could enter. Passage through the cliffs was unlikely, yet the possibility existed; and if we were seen, it would force us to leave for another place. The camp was always vulnerable, and we all maintained established rules to keep our cover intact.

Up in the mountains my rehabilitation progressed quickly. My sight was restored in a few days, which gave me strong incentive to recover. The vigorous physical training didn't start until September, when I began jujitsu and boxing with Vasil, at forty a veteran of World War II.

Vasil grew up in Prokopyevsk, in the Sayan Mountains of the Soviet Union; he studied history at Astrakhan University, north of the Caspian Sea. Shortly before his graduation, the Soviet infantry drafted him and trained him in espionage; among other skills, he learned how to kill with his bare hands. Vasil was a deserter from the Red Army. He had joined the 1944 German retreat; then he deserted again, seeking refuge in the Bohemian mountains, where he joined the first partisans that formed after the Soviets occupied Czechoslovakia.

Training with him daily, I prepared for my final direct assignment in the Czech Resistance, scheduled for the end of October, in Slovakia.

My exposure to the authorities through my imprisonment rendered me useless for further undercover activity. After this assignment, I would have to choose whether to stay in the mountains and participate in commando raids or go into exile.

Possible fallout from the prison rescue no longer preoccupied Pavel. The Communists in Czechoslovakia had made no arrests in connection with the breakout; Pavel and his commandos had struck quickly, and left no trace. Their clothing, boots, gloves, masks, and weapons had been stored in the mountain hideouts, and were not to be used in action again to avoid recognition. An extensive search by communist agents to find the perpetrators and punish them had, so far, been unsuccessful.

This left Pavel, during the following two months, to focus on a long-standing attempt to connect with Polish counterparts. To appreciate Pavel's plan, one must remember that to the western Allies, the Soviet occupation of eastern European nations was legal, and thus beyond the scope of the Allies' concerns. Not so to the persecuted people in those countries. Each Soviet satellite had its own underground organization, and each accomplished significant acts against Communists, but not enough to make resistance visible to the West.

Pavel hoped to unite all the organizations into one force, as it had been during World War II. A coalition seemed the only viable solution, the only way to gain enough impact to capture the West's attention. He believed that by joining the Slovak and Hungarian Resistance with us, the Polish would follow. He hoped—as did we all—that the Baltic nations and Bulgaria and Romania would join as well, since they all wished to be independent from the Soviet Union. It was time for the Eastern European countries to stop the Soviet Union's domination in the area; such unity would send a powerful message to the Soviets and to the world.

None knew how this political interaction might end, or how the participation of all these small countries in the struggle for freedom would appeal to their individual national character. I thought that freedom would be the strongest motivational force in the minds of people subjected to tyranny; freedom thus had to soar as a priority in the unification movement. I later found that this was not so, and that people's outlooks on life changed to suit their individual needs, influenced too often by the bitter nationalistic chauvinism that plagued them for centuries. This pride divided them, and the Soviets took advantage of it, feeding people with socialistic ideals that were purely superficial. The disagreements and the power struggle among individual leaders in these small nations, even within the resistance itself, became ever more costly as such partisanship allowed the Soviets to continue to enslave us all.

Making contact with the Slovak-Hungarian underground for Pavel was my responsibility, since I knew the man with two crucial connections: one was to the Slovak underground and the other was to the Hungarians. I could pass for a native in either country, since I spoke both languages fluently.

Before my arrest, Pavel instructed me to set up a safe meeting with the Slovak underground and to possibly engage the Hungarian underground leaders, as well. Now Pavel wanted me to finish the project. But to approach anyone involved in the resistance meant endless complications and risks; Pavel ordered this operation to be safe, guarding our interests as well as those of the Slovaks, who were exposed to the same hard-line government surveillance as we were.

Training grew daily more important for me; with a renewed assignment, boredom vanished and I longed for action, longed to be away from this lonely place. Physical strength was a critical component of my skills. I knew that my mission in Slovakia involved many obstacles and a high probability of confrontations with well-trained enemy agents; the country was full of them.

The idea of an encounter with them frightened me, because I knew they were the best in the business. If my recent experience with crude interrogators had cost me so much, what more might I have to endure from true "experts"? I remembered my uncle saying that the only defense against them was to avoid them, if possible. The Soviets had exported hundreds of these men to the satellite countries; they scattered them among the civilian population to spy, gain people's confidence, and to trick the unsuspecting into a web of political intrigue. The Communists became ever more keenly alert, determined to stop the resistance at all cost. Our work was becoming increasingly dangerous.

Vasil spoke little, because his Czech and German were poor, but what he did say impressed me deeply. He made me memorize the description of a typical Soviet agent; it was almost identical to the one my uncle had given me previously and, in fact, described Vasil himself perfectly.

"So, they look like you, then," I said.

"Ta-da! Remember that. It is important that you recognize your enemy before he recognizes you," Vasil replied as he walked away. Then he snapped at me over his shoulder, "You better be ready for me tomorrow, for you must overpower me and knock the hell out of me."

I did not think I could ever learn how to do that. Still, I thought I was physically ready for the mission, given all the hard work I had done to prime myself. Had I not been swimming in lakes and rivers with strong currents? Had I not nearly perfected my martial arts training?

However, Vasil was not so confident; he urged Pavel to scrap the mission.

"He can't kill a fly," he said.

"He may get lucky; perhaps he won't have to," Pavel responded. "And we have nobody else who knows that territory. He must go."

I made every effort to set aside my fears of the enemy and, in truth, I did not let concerns about the future bother me much. Unknown adventure lay ahead; that was all. At the moment, I was worried about how many more punches from Vasil I would have to endure. My other concern involved the upcoming treatments I'd require to conceal my identity. Several painful injections in the face and chin were needed. I did not know what the substance was, but it would dissipate in three or four weeks. The intense discomfort from it would remain for a long time though. With a different haircut and the coloring in my face altered, I would be unrecognizable. I also learned a new walk, changed my way of speaking and gesturing, and above all, I changed my voice itself by chewing special caramels provided by Dr. Podlipný.

Pavel supervised my transformation and gave me final instructions. That afternoon, a cosmetologist and the doctor came to alter my appearance.

After all the preparations, I was set.

THE LAST JOB FOR MY COUNTRY

We spent days discussing the details of Pavel's plan and made last-minute revisions. Pavel evaluated the odds and decided it was the right time to proceed.

In the late afternoon on the day before my departure to Slovakia, we sat near a small mountain stream talking about the accomplishments of our organization. They had tapered off to merely gathering and transferring news to the west. Serious political espionage lacked the participation of the other satellites and the Allies; the resistance limited its involvement to receiving intelligence for its own political purposes and publications. Pavel regarded this stifled activity as a threat to our organization's effectiveness in achieving eventual liberation from the Soviets.

"We must get through to the Slovaks somehow," said Pavel.

"We've got to," I replied, wincing. My new face hurt, and I felt as if the pain, not the injections, disfigured my features. "I trust my contact, and through him, I can't fail."

"It's hard to gamble on one ace, though," Pavel said.

"Yes, but he's never failed me before," I responded.

"If they catch you, that's it; I won't even know where they'll keep you before they kill you," said Pavel. "I will not be able to help you, for you'll be dead."

"Don't worry. My contact is good. He has power and money, and he will help me arrange everything."

"I won't talk about your mission; I'll just set up a safe place for you two to meet. I hope they'll trust you; you're so young, and that may not inspire their confidence."

"Remember that the old man will be with me," I said referring to my dear friend Professor Zenaty. "And he will help me approach our Slovakian and Hungarian counterparts."

"Yes . . . but the others you will deal with are hard, self-centered, and ruthless...and each wants his own glory." Pavel paused, and we both watched a bubbling stream for a while without speaking. Then he broke the silence, saying, "They would tear you to pieces. Cover your ass and duck in time. You will be unarmed and alone. I hope the pain in your face will keep you alert."

"Don't worry," I said. "I know the place and people, and I know where to go if I need something. Remember, they're also eager to break the silence and to talk with us."

"True," Pavel acknowledged. "But they are also incurably independent, and they'll do anything for a bit of fame." After another short pause, he asked, "How do you feel? Physically, I mean? Are you up for this?"

"I am ready, and I am leaving tomorrow as scheduled. I have even been chewing on Podlipný's candy for several days to change my voice." I stuck out my tongue at him; on it lay a colorless pellet.

"I'd noticed it was changing. You have begun to sound like a woman. I hope it's not permanent," Pavel said with a wry smile.

Later on, after supper, I walked to my cabin and wrote a few lines to my parents. I sealed the letter and marked it for Pavel to give them in case I did not come back. I brought it to Vasil for safekeeping and then went to bed.

From the cabin I watched the dark cliff that rose high above the hills and began to think about my assignment. My assumed identity for this mission was Karel Syvák, age twenty-five, part-time history student at Charles University and book salesman for the Prague Publishing Company. The changes to my face made me appear older than I really was.

My assignment would lead me to southern Slovakia, where I was born twenty years before. I had to meet an old, retired, and wealthy gentleman in his villa on the outskirts of Lučenec.

Mr. František Ženatý was a historian, and was now a strong promoter of good books. From 1935 to 1939, he had been a professor of history in the secondary school known as Rimavská Sobota Gymnasium. An inheritance from his father made him independently wealthy, and during the Nazi occupation he had been a strong supporter of the Slovak freedom fighters. The war reduced his assets, but in the socialistic paradise he was still considered a capitalist and was thus a *persona non grata*. He became a strong supporter of the Slovak underground.

I knew Professor Ženatý well, for he and my father had been close friends since 1922. I revered them both; I loved my father, but Professor Ženatý ranked close with him.

The following morning—Saturday, October 23, 1948—I used the same one-horse buggy that had brought me to that secluded spot in the lonely hills. I drove about twenty kilometers away from the hills toward Prachatice. I left the horse and buggy with a contact and then, by rail, arrived in Lučenec in three days' time.

My attire as a book salesman fit well, but had wrinkled during the three days of travel. On the dusty road from the station it was too hot; I loosened my tie and changed my briefcase from hand to hand several times. I looked forward to relaxing at my friend's home.

The isolated and fenced house sat on a plain between a small hill I just passed and an old cargo track behind the river Ipel. To my right stood a large field, and to my left were many acres of wooded land. In front of the house was parked a late model Škoda; I recognized it as an official vehicle belonging to a government agency. In that moment I knew I was in trouble; yet it was too late, for I was too close and must have been seen.

A young man answered the door when I knocked, and my heart skipped more than a beat. The man I saw resembled Vasil, and I knew that could mean only one thing. Still, I had to remain calm.

"I am Karel Syvák from Prague Publishing. I think that Mr. Ženatý is expecting me," I said, bowing courteously.

"Please follow me," answered the man as he showed me to the library.

I knew the house in detail, and searched my mind for a way out. The door to the library was open. My suspicion was accurate; such agents always worked in pairs. There was no doubt; they were from the KGB, and my old friend the professor had already been seized. I was in it up to my neck, but was able to overcome my fear and maintain self-control.

Quickly sizing up their advantage, I chose swift action: keeping a step ahead of them. I looked innocent and convincing enough, but I also knew I could not measure up physically, not even to one of them; they were about five years older, and clearly stronger. I would have to outsmart them instead.

"Good afternoon, sir," I said as I stepped close to the desk, where another man like the first sat. He was just finishing lunch and had a bottle of wine before him on his right; in his right hand he held a full glass.

"He is right-handed," I thought, hoping to detect even the slightest clue of how such a man might be beaten.

"What can I do for you?" he asked.

"I am Karel Syvák from Prague Publishing Company," I answered. "I have brought some book covers that Mr. Ženatý ordered."

I stepped around the desk to his right, and before he could say anything, I opened the portfolio that lay on the desk. The man switched his glass to his left hand while the other man stepped out, closing the door behind him. I was certain he wanted to check to see whether I was alone or not. When the man at the desk placed his glass on the table and I placed the briefcase in front of him, my left arm covered his view for a split second. With my right hand, I grabbed the wine bottle and crushed the man's forehead with it in one fast and powerful stroke; then I jumped to the side of the door. When the other man, attracted by the noise, stuck his head into the room, I used the blow that Vasil had taught me on his neck. As he straightened up from the pain, I tore his Adam's apple with a right hook and let him collapse on the floor. I went to the desk, closed the book cover portfolio, took one of the revolvers and extra ammunition from the men's pockets, and gulped down some leftover food and wine. Then I grabbed the car keys and walked out.

Slowly, I drove the car to the end of the road behind the orchard, shifted to low gear, jumped out, and let it coast into the river. I heard the last gurgle from the sinking car as I crossed the elevated pedestrian bridge toward the old rail line. I vanished behind the cargo cars and walked to a single track where trains of boxcars frequently passed; one, at a snail's pace, was heading toward Rimavská Sobota, which was about fifteen kilometers away. I jumped aboard, lay on the flatbed, and evaluated my situation as calmly as I could.

Vasil came immediately to mind. He had thought I couldn't do it. I mumbled to myself, terrified, "Jesus, Mary . . . did I kill them? I'll never know for sure . . . but that was a close one. Too close."

I checked the revolver, put all the extra ammunition in my left pocket and tried to relax, but I could not. I knew that, at least for now, the Slovaks were out of my reach, and that Mr. Ženatý was in deep trouble; it seemed unlikely that I would ever see that dear, kind old man again. My mission had failed, and who knew how gravely this would set back Pavel's plans. I knew I was not safe; in a few hours the police would be everywhere. I reasoned that I had to get to Hungary, which was just a few kilometers to the southeast. I could see the horizon of the low plain; but to cross it was nearly impossible.

The train approached the outskirts of the Rimavská Sobota station; still traveling slowly, it crossed dozens of exchanges and rail ramps. I chose one and jumped off, then bypassed the town on foot, crossing the large fields, now dry and bare in the October sun. To my left, I saw Etelka's father's orchard in the distance. I passed farmers as they turned over the soil with one-horse plows, holding onto the wobbling handles, harness yoke, and whip all at the same time; they were oblivious to what was happening around them.

After reaching the outskirts of the town and dodging the busy city park, I came to the eastern side of Rimavská Sobota at about 2:00 p.m. Unseen in the shade of the orchard trees, I came to Etelka's old gazebo and hid myself there. I stretched out on a wooden bench imagining the girl I could have married, and whom I had only seen once since 1938, and that was only for a brief two-week visit just after the war. My mind was overwhelmed with questions: How was she now? Had she changed? Could I trust her? Was she influenced by the new communist doctrine being fed wholesale to the young? How was she affected by the news of my execution a few weeks prior? Would my new appearance confuse her?

I recalled how Etelka's mother had counted on a wedding, but my own mother had been against it. She pointed out to us how difficult it would be to live in a society that expected us to be of the same nationality. My mother spoke, of course, from painful experience. Etelka's parents became angry earlier in the year when I disappeared without explanation, leaving their plans for us dangling; they probably heard of my supposed execution from my sister, and this must have confused them. None of this really mattered, however; although Etelka and I liked each other as friends, and though we did a little experimenting and exploring, we never wanted to marry. We remained solely friends.

I drifted off in the midst of my musings. Suddenly I awoke, startled; exhausted as I was, I had dozed off on the wooden bench of the gazebo. A dog licking my face and my hand had awakened me; it was Papo, Etelka's dog, who nuzzled me and whimpered. I embraced the old dog with my left arm as I observed the activity in Etelka's house. I had to be cautious; for me, this was hostile territory no matter how well the dog received me. I would have to approach Etelka and her family carefully, not knowing their situation.

It was after 6:00 p.m., around dinnertime, and daylight had just begun to fade. I had to speak with Etelka; she could help me to escape to Hungary and hide me in one of the remote refuges we both used to know. If the two men in Mr. Ženatý's house had survived, my description would be all over Slovakia; if they had died, an angry group of KGB agents would be searching for an unknown individual who had eliminated two trained men. Professor Ženatý, if still alive, had probably suffered terrible torture; he may have already disclosed my identity, but not knowing my disguise, his confession would be uncertain.

I had to dispose of the briefcase without a trace; I also needed a change of clothing, some food, and the means to disappear somehow for a while. Etelka could help.

I left the gazebo and peered through a window, where I saw the housekeeper washing dishes and Etelka playing the piano in the study. I saw her parents leave for a walk.

"All clear," I thought, and I entered Etelka's room with Papo at my side. I grabbed her from behind so she could not scream. She looked at the dog, not understanding why he didn't attack the stranger. I explained quickly, and when she calmed down I showed her the birthmark above my left knee. That convinced her, and she was ready to listen.

"I need you," I said urgently. "I'll wait for you in the old mill near the pumping station. I'll be behind the wheel at the river bank."

Though still startled and gasping for air, she understood. "I don't know how fast I can get there, so be patient," she said.

"I need a change of clothing and some food."

"No problem. I'll be there as soon as I can."

"Invent some smart story to tell the housekeeper, and have her explain it to your parents so they won't look for me."

"Don't worry. I'll take care of everything," Etelka said quietly as she watched me walk out.

At the gazebo I picked up the briefcase and left for the river through the small orchards. At the pumping station I removed from the briefcase a small leather bag with a first-aid kit, a shaving knife, and soap; I stuffed these things inside my shirt. Then I filled the briefcase with stones and slipped it into a large sewer sedimentation tank.

The wheel of the mill on the riverbank, overgrown by wild bushes and tall grass, stuck out on its rusty shaft like a torture wheel in prison; but this one did not turn. I sat on the weathered concrete base of the axle and evaluated my chances of getting out safely.

"This place is a trap," I thought, remembering Vasil's words, *Cover your ass and don't trust anyone.* It would be better off for me to be farther away and able to oversee the spot.

Ashamed of not trusting my own friend, I climbed on top of the wall to see the site. It was getting dark quickly; the river was lined with heavy growth on both sides, and the orchards to my left were the darkest. The walls and near side of the park on the other side of the river, to my right, were illuminated by streetlights. A large green meadow between the orchards and the river lay immediately before me; I could clearly see if someone would approach from there.

However, with dogs, they could find me anywhere.

Upstream in a small clearing I spotted what appeared to be a small boat. I walked up the riverbank, passing the old mill, and then climbed into the boat and drifted back down, passing the old mill again and drifting lower to the bridge. I hid the tiny boat and stepped onto an elevated edge, from where I could see the mill, the bridge, and the open field separating the city from its outskirts. I did not think dogs could trace me here, and I knew I could drift farther downstream in the boat, if need be. I went through my whole scheme in my mind again, and then sat leaning against an old trunk, taking a much needed rest. The hunger and fatigue numbed the pain in my cheeks, and I dozed off as I waited for Etelka and whatever else was to come.

ON THE RUN

The night breeze from the river chilled me to the bone, while the sharp, radiating pain in my face woke me sporadically. Exhaustion had caught up with me, but I forced myself to stay as alert as I could. I felt hopeless, lonely, and dejected. I was running like a hunted fox, friendless, likely pursued by dogs. I believed my capture was near; it was just a question of time. My fear of my pursuers kept me just a few steps ahead—so far.

Etelka finally appeared on the bank walking downstream, bypassing the pumping station. She carried a bag; it seemed as if it must be heavy, for she changed it frequently from one hand to another. Upon reaching the old mill, she disappeared in the shadow of the old building. There was no sign of anyone following her. I walked toward the mill wheel along the creeping trees and the wild bush at the riverbank, until I could see her profile. She was at the same spot where I had sat before. At the tree trunk I stood up as high as I could to check around, and then I approached her.

"I couldn't manage it any faster," she whispered. "I am truly sorry. I was terrified for you. Here, eat now."

"No," I said. "We'll go to another spot." I picked up the bag and motioned to her to follow. Reaching the anchored boat, I pulled her down and then asked her to pass me the food.

125

"I have bad news," she said as she handed me a morsel. "Something unusual has provoked the police and the communist secretariat."

"Why the Party?" I wondered aloud.

"My parents were talking about a rumor that the police and the Party had a shakeup. Some said that the NKVD is in on it; they have agents all over. Railway stations, border crossings, hotels, and even the movie theaters have been staked out, as if they are searching for somebody."

"Then crossing to Hungary would be impossible?" I asked.

"It's out of the question, and even if we were to make it across, we would face the same conditions there," she said.

"What about some distant farmhouse or other hideaway?"

"They would pick you up in no time. I actually think you would be safest right here in town."

"What on earth do you mean?"

She told me what had happened when the Slovak Communist Party took over the old city hall about a year before. They argued with the police about it; both wanted to have their headquarters in the historic structure. The Russians resolved it for them; the NKVD took it over and neither the Party nor the police were able to use the space.

"You know what? They don't even call themselves NKVD. They hung up a sign: Committee for Internal Affairs. Then they threw everyone else out. I think you would be safest in that building," explained Etelka.

"You must be out of your mind," I said.

"I am sure they would feel the same way, but until this excitement blows over, you could quite safely watch all the commotion from the second floor, right above the NKVD chief's office."

"How do you know about all of this?" I asked.

"My friend, an old border patrolman, who helps me come and go to Hungary where I attend school, was summoned to a hearing one day. The NKVD checked all state employees for competence and reliability; they liked him and they hired his wife to clean their offices. She told me once that the second floor is completely empty."

"You mean to tell me that she could get me through?"

"I don't think she could, but I will," said Etelka, sounding determined.

"How?"

"Leave it to me. You'll be safe. Tonight, you'll stay under the stage in the park, and tomorrow, in the late afternoon when the park is full of people, I'll walk with you to the city hall. At this point, you really have no choice. Besides, a large crowd is the safest place for you."

I realized she was right. Her idea was more than clever, and I thought we could use someone like her in Bohemia.

I finished eating, disrobed, and washed in the river; shaving was hard on my numbed face. I rolled all my extra clothing firmly around a large stone, submerged it, and placed other stones over it below the water's surface. We then waited another hour to avoid any late walkers before going to the park.

Poorly illuminated, the deserted public grounds were restful in the shadows of the chestnuts and acacias. The stage gazebo stood in the dark, and the opening to the substructure in the back was invisible; it was used for the storage of old chairs and benches, and a roof kept the stage and substage dry. Behind the wall at the opening, I found four flat benches on which I could sleep.

"Nobody will bother you here," Etelka said. "This place is so dirty and smells so bad that not even desperate lovers would use it."

A chuckle escaped me. "You've gotten me the most luxurious accommodations available, eh?"

She ignored my comment and continued, "You'll have to hide during the day, and at 4:00 p.m. I'll come and walk you downtown. Until then you'll have sufficient food."

"How did you explain your absence to your parents?"

"I arranged it with our housekeeper; she'll cover for me." She paused. "Would you like me to . . . stay with you for a while?"

"Yes. Yes, I would," I replied, thinking back to earlier times and our innocent explorations. So much had changed. I had to explain to her what happened to me in prison, when the guards tortured and crushed me; desire had been a stranger to me since then. Still, Etelka stayed with me, and we talked long into the evening as her tender embrace warmed me inside and out. Her understanding about communist atrocities showed how her remarkable maturity had grown since I had seen her last. Late at night, she finally returned home.

The park remained deserted until the next day at noon, when an occasional nanny pushing a baby buggy appeared. By 3:00 p.m. the broad, paved walks had filled with hundreds of people just walking, talking, and listening to Gypsy music.

Etelka came on time.

"Listen," she said. "We can't be seen together. Many people know me and would question who I walk with. You must go alone on the main boulevard and I'll meet you on the Red Square by the clock."

"I'll be there," I said, leaving the substage. Moving with the crowd I realized why Etelka's reasoning was accurate; I looked around, amazed, and for the first time since leaving Pavel's hideout, I felt safe. The promenade was jammed with people of all ages in groups, shopping and having fun. In the crowd, I was anonymous.

Etelka waited at the clock with a food-packed basket on her arm. Spotting me in the busy street, she approached, smiling, and handed me the basket as if we were on our usual daily shopping tour. Then she grabbed my other arm and led me by a side street to the rear of the old city hall building. We stopped in a vestibule leading to a narrow concrete stairway, where she motioned for me to wait. She tiptoed barefoot down to a steel door, listened, and gestured for me to follow quickly. Stagnant air filled the cool subterranean space of the medieval building; its limestone blocks were sweating condensed water droplets from the moist air and the surface was stained with textured streaks. The corroded steel door frame, shedding heavy rust flakes, was held onto the stone wall by flimsy plates thinned by age. Not that long before, I had seen basements like this.

Etelka pushed the door open just enough for us to enter. To the left, half-empty coal bins held some coke and stacked, broken furniture. In the center stood a large coal burner for the central heating, installed recently to improve conditions for the new tenants. On the floor to the right, behind the door through which we entered, lay three unfinished pine board boxes that looked disturbingly like coffins. I froze momentarily; the three boxes made my mind race, filling it with the image of the two men I suspected I had killed, and of the absent Professor Ženatý. Tags bearing Moscow addresses, attached to two of the boxes, verified my suspicions. While I shivered at having my anxieties confirmed, I also felt relief that I could not be identified. It was clear that the NKVD did not have an office in Lučenec; the headquarters for this region were in Rimavská Sobota.

I was afraid to look in the third box, which did not have a tag. Trembling slightly, I opened the lid, paused, and felt myself overwhelmed with grief and years of memories. It was my friend Professor Ženatý. The poor old man; they had tortured him, and he bore the awful marks of it.

Devastated by the discovery, I followed Etelka up another narrow stairway to the second floor, which offered more than four hundred square meters of empty area.

"Who were they?" Etelka asked. "Did you know them?"

I could not respond, so she went on to explain the layout of the second floor.

"This corridor cuts the second floor in half and is parallel to the Red Square on your right. Windows on your left overlook the alleys and the side streets. There is only one toilet you can use, at the far end to your left, and you must flush it only around 1:00 p.m., after lunch, when many people use the toilets on the first floor. You must be totally quiet during daytime hours; don't walk, because some areas of the floor move and falling dust could alert someone to your presence."

I surveyed the area carefully and chose the room on my left, close to the narrow stairs where we had just entered and with a window to the alley.

The Red Square clock struck 5:00 p.m. We had to wait for several hours before everything on the first floor calmed down. Nobody could see us—and we could see nothing outside, since the windows were covered with a thick dust. With my fingertip I made a peephole on the glass to observe the Square. Sitting on the wooden floor and talking softly about the old days, Etelka and I resumed our discussion of yesterday and continued to fill each other in about the past and present. She couldn't get over the news about the prison I had been in, and she told me about many atrocities committed by the Communists in both Slovakia and Hungary. She felt sorry for my family, having to live with the notion of me being dead.

As we sat and talked, I remembered my Uncle Joe. He had hidden like this from the Gestapo in 1942; he lived on the upper floor above their headquarters in Brno, and had been safe there for several months. Now the same thing was happening to me, and I wondered how long I would have to hide in plain sight.

When everyone on the first floor finally left, I cut the floor insulation above the chief's office so I could see and hear better. "Maybe tomorrow I'll be able to overhear them," I said.

From the Red Square faint lights from the streetlamps penetrated the dirty glass. Etelka needed to return home and was about to go, but suddenly a car came to a noisy stop in front of the building. Several men boisterously entered the chief's office, gesticulating and arguing; instinctively, I grabbed my revolver. Listening in, I understood them talking about shipping the two boxes in the basement to the Bratislava airport, some four hours away, from where an airliner would take them to Moscow. Somebody had to drive to the airport as soon as possible, because the flight was scheduled to leave at 9:00 a.m. the next day. The man in charge agreed to order some of the foreign service employees to drive out to the airport by no later than 2:00 a.m.

An outrageous idea crossed my mind, and at once I decided to go through with it: I was going to change places with one of the KGB agents in the box. It would be uncomfortable, but it would be worth the risk; it would enable me to reach the airport without being seen. This might be my only chance to escape. Etelka agreed to help and would nail the box top shut. I told her to only use four nails, so that I would be able to get out easily when I had to do so.

We walked to the pitch-dark basement by feeling the humid walls. With my knife I opened one of the tagged boxes, lifted the body over my shoulder, and buried it in a coal bin. I stacked the broken furniture on top of it and removed the sheet that had covered the body, for it stank. I stuffed that into the furnace. Then I drilled several air holes in the box ends and tried it on for size. It was tight; I was 5'10" tall, so I had to bend my knees a little.

We left the casket to air out, for it smelled terrible; they hadn't even washed the dead agent, just applied formaldehyde on him. We climbed the stairs to the second floor, going there to relax as we waited until 1:00 a.m., when I had to be sealed in the box. I found it a challenge to be calm; I had to stop drinking wine to avoid exhaling its smell, and I couldn't eat, for I was sickened by the stench of formaldehyde vapor.

At about 1:30 a.m., shortly after Etelka finished nailing the box cover over me, three men came. I could hear their chatter; they were Slovaks, employees of the NKVD. From their conversation I could understand that two of them would drive a small truck to Bratislava. Etelka, hiding behind the coal burner, watched them take the two boxes up to the loading dock. When they carried me up the stairs I slid backward in the box, crushing my head against the board. As my neck twisted against the hard box I got an agonizing cramp in my chin, which radiated down to my neck muscle and momentarily paralyzed me. I held back a scream and just hoped they would not drop me; the impact would break my neck.

They pushed the box on the truck bed feet first, and in a few minutes the truck moved on. The canvas, tied to the sides and top of the truck, flapped furiously in the wind. I began to have second thoughts about using this way out. My stiff and confined condition bothered me; being closed up in the box for five hours now seemed preposterous. In a little while it felt nigh unbearable; the sickeningly sweet smell of death nauseated me, and the phobia of being trapped in a small space tested my endurance even more. I remembered the prison cell nights, especially after I lost my vision, and my muscles contracted in throbbing spasms. Restlessness, panic, and hysteria came upon me; I grew frantic. I forced my mouth closer to the left hole in the board to suck some air; it helped, but not for long. The darkness and confinement, as in the prison cell, began to affect my mind. I had enough air, yet I could not breathe; I could move my hands and feet, yet I felt compressed by the hard boards until it seemed my lungs were squeezing my heart like a vise.

The phobia grew, and I started to lose control. The horrible contest between body and psyche pulled me apart, and I was unsure how long I would be able to distinguish between pain and cramps, or how long I would be able to tolerate the darkness and confinement. From time to time the poke of my revolver, which I had taken from the NKVD man in the professor's house and placed under my sensitive chin, kept me alert. I heard the two drivers talking, but their words fused with the monotonous rattle of the truck. With my finger I felt the side of the wooden box, which by now had gathered slimy deposits formed by the vapor of my sweat.

To distract myself, I imagined Etelka taking her basket and, unseen in the sleeping city, walking home. I saw her amused that they had not actually killed me as had been reported a few weeks before, when my sister called her to explain about my assumed name; like everything else in our godforsaken land, the news was false. I could almost hear her giggling. She probably could not sleep, and early the next day would take Papo downtown on his leash, hoping to hear more news.

A bump of some kind made the truck jump, and my distraction faded unexpectedly. I found myself in darkness again, short on air, cramped, and phobic. The sudden and violent jolt bounced me from side to side and brought me abruptly to an unbearable state of mind that I could not repress. Just short of falling into an abyss of madness, unable to bear the pressure on me any longer, I used all the strength I could muster and broke off the lid.

Both the driver and partner gaped over their shoulders in shock at the opened coffin and the half-erect body aiming a revolver at them. The driver's grip on the wheel froze the truck's direction and it ran straight into a ditch and a tree, where the rubble of twisted metal and flesh fused together. Both men died instantly, but I, protected by the box during the crash, was spared. Unharmed, save for some bruises and abrasions, I climbed out from the wreckage.

It was around 4:30 a.m. and quite dark, but to my left over a tall mountain range, I could see traces of light in the east, indicating that we had traveled south; the large river in the deep valley had to be the Hron, and it flowed south. The mountains on the east side of the river rose high, which explained the darkness. The deserted road had no identification signs save those that warned of curves. I had to assume I was heading toward Bratislava. The wreck would not be seen until daylight, which gave me a couple hours head start.

To mislead dogs, should the authorities try to find the missing corpse, I covered my shoes with gasoline that slowly dripped from the damaged fuel tank; then I tiptoed barefoot to the paved road, put on the shoes again, and walked north for about a kilometer. There I could see a large bridge over the river.

I left the road and climbed down closer to the stream. From there, looking north, I saw the lights of a small village; I wondered which village it was. The bridge, quite prominent even in the dark, was not too inviting for a fugitive. I decided to stay away from it, and observed the river conditions to see whether I could drift downstream to get a few kilometers away from the crash site. By the riverbank I found many boats, but all of them were chained and padlocked; to take one surely would have shown my trail, so I kept looking and walking the bank for more than two kilometers, passing by several cottages.

I came to a large stream coming from the west that merged with the river. At a short distance to the southwest I spotted a few lights from another village. My watch showed 5:30 a.m.; shortly it would be daybreak. I walked quickly up the stream, dodged the village, crossed the main road about four kilometers south from the crash site, and found a trail behind a sign for the village Zamovica. I hoped the trail would be the pass between the high peaks of Vtáčník to the north and Trebič to the south.

My memory and knowledge of geography came in handy, and in nine hours I reached Chinorany. From there—via cargo train, the safest transportation—I passed through Trenčín and Vsetín en route to Valašské Meziříčí, where I wanted to see my parents; they had resided there since the end of the war.

Etelka's smoked sausage had kept me from starving, but I desperately needed a bath; I wasn't fit to go among people, for my clothing, Etelka's father's shirt and pants, was filthy. I surveyed the rail yard and passenger station from my cargo wagon through a fissure in the sliding door; at the rear of the station I noticed a public toilet, but I couldn't go there without being noticed. To step out of my wagon without attracting attention would be difficult; I would have to wait until dark, and even then I couldn't reach the toilet. However, I located some passenger wagons on the sidetrack, at a fair distance from the loading platform. There, in one of the lavatories, I found sufficient water in the supply pipe to wash and shave; I still carried the shaving knife and cream I'd earlier stashed under my shirt. Later I returned to the cargo wagon, which was shifted onto the inactive track, to try to sleep; but I just dozed, awakening frequently from noises in the night.

Early before dawn, I lifted myself through the roof hatch to see the terrain behind the tracks, where I had to cross to reach the outskirts of the town. Most of the rail workers started work at 7:00 a.m.; it seemed prudent for me to leave with the sunrise, just in case some employee showed up early. The overcrowded marketplace where I was heading offered the safest refuge, for there I could mingle without drawing attention.

It was strange coming to my old town secretly, with such a changed appearance. The streets were deserted. The post office opened at 8:00 a.m.; I had to wait in the plaza until 8:30 a.m.; at which time people filled the small post office, making me inconspicuous. I needed to send a telegram to Pavel's Pilsen post office box to let him know I was alive; it was October 29, and if he didn't receive a message from me by October 31, he would assume I had been caught.

While waiting for the post office to open I walked here and there, keeping a low profile on the busy square—memories of my parents and their friends, many of whom were now gone, having fallen prey to the perils of our times. On the square, time stopped; or perhaps I was too quickly remembering, holding everything around me motionless.

Suddenly I spotted my mother, simply dressed but still attractive and elegant, crossing the market square with a shopping basket on her arm, just steps away from where I aimlessly roamed. She passed me many times in the market, and later at the newsstand; my face burned with pain as I held back a sob and stifled a cry, for she bumped into me while turning from a market counter and did not recognize me. She apologized softly; I saw pain in her eyes masked by a smile, and I suspected she must have compared me to the son she had lost. I wanted to embrace her and show her I was alive; I wanted to stop her grief by explaining everything, but I could not, for it would not be safe for either of us. Then she stopped for a daily paper and turned onto a side street that led to her home.

How cruel our situation had become. Weeping, I returned to the post office. I dried my face and sent the telegram to Pavel. Then I walked to the rail yard to catch a cargo train toward Pilsen. Avoiding the loading platform, I climbed into a boxcar with a roof hatch; a roof opening was essential in case the train attendants latched the sliding door during their rounds.

The ride on such trains was slow and gave me time to think. My life was overwhelmed by wars, hunger, hiding, and running.

And I was growing weary.

Then my uncle's advice after the uprising in Prague came to me. He had told me to join Pavel in Bohemia, and that if the resistance failed, I should go into exile.

"Change your nationality," he said. "Change your name. Change everything, and build a new life for yourself. Establish a new family in a land that will give you freedom."

My own land was hostile, and I was now a fugitive, lonely and confused, who was in dire need of help and advice.

It was time for me to heed my uncle's words.

The monotonous click of the boxcar's wheels reminded me of my flight. Avoiding stations, loading platforms, and waiting rooms, I changed trains at the rear of the tracks, staying alert. Often I missed connections, because I did not know the schedule and did not want to risk discovery by trying to find out, but slowly I approached my destination by using the cargo lines for two days and nights. Finally, I reached Pavel's camp in the Bohemian forest, and they knew I was coming.

Vasil waited; he didn't ask any questions. "When you are ready," he said. "We will talk." We did just that, long into the night.

Pavel was greatly disappointed, and I understood why.

"Who knows," he said. "This may have been the last chance for us to try this. Now, though, you have to get out of here. In a few days your face will change back again, and you will be useless in the streets and unable to do undercover work."

I stretched out on a cot, reviewing my recent adventures, which even to me felt unreal. I would never forget the terror of the dark confined box, which tested my endurance and my fear of dying. Why should I be frightened of dying? I did not know what death truly was; no one did. Who had made dying a bad word? Yes, it was universally considered awful—unwanted, painful, feared—because when it happened it stopped us from moving and being, and we interpreted that as if something had ended. But what if it were actually a beautiful experience? What if, with death, something actually began instead?

I had to come to terms with death somehow, for it would be always at my heels from that moment on. I could not fear it.

In the midst of pondering these deep and dark ideas, I wondered what my father would think or do. I wished he were there so I could ask him.

five

THE TIME BETWEEN

I was born near a border
and crossing others became common.
Sometimes the crossing
was an arduous journey,
through treacherous mountains
protected by fierce dogs and bloodthirsty guards.
Sometimes it was an escape.

ANOTHER ESCAPE

I WAS TWENTY YEARS old when I had to flee my native land.

If I had stayed, I would have been killed. It was as simple and as terrible as that.

I loved Czechoslovakia, and that feeling was stronger than almost anything else I knew; yet the urge for self-preservation drove me to leave, hoping to return when the madness ended.

In the meantime, I would continue to fight while in exile. The years away might be difficult, but the whole world would open up to me, and I would experience things I had not known before. I would make the

United States my home, and would find freedom there until the day I could find it once more in my own country.

As I awaited Pavel's instructions, I considered the journey ahead. Crossing the border near Vimperk, in the Bohemian forest, would not be difficult—or so I thought, having already passed over so many borders. The bitter adventure in the hills and a potential upcoming and serious meeting with Americans kept in my mind that a demanding part of my war was nigh; my job would be to convince the Americans in Bavaria that we in Czechoslovakia were dedicated to fighting the Soviets in any way we could, and we expected help.

I knew the United States Congress did not allow interference in other nations' internal affairs, so I was not sure how the meeting would end. Still, Pavel had assigned me as a liaison to the United States Civil Intelligence Corps (CIC), knowing I had the right experience, background, and skills; I had fought in the resistance for many years, had devised a new communication procedure that eluded the enemy's probing, and was fluent in German, Hungarian, Russian, Czech, Slovak, and Polish. If anyone could persuade the Americans, it was I.

I could only hope for the best.

I had to wait for Pavel's go-ahead and good weather before crossing into Bohemia. Three young men would be crossing the hills with me.

Finally, we got word that we were to cross the border on November 12, 1948. The young men accompanying me were named Tonda, Lojza, and Mirek. Among us I was the only one associated with the Bohemian underground, but Mirek was a close friend; we called each other brothers.

In the late afternoon, deep in the wilderness between the frontier of the Bohemian forest, the steep cliffs of Kniežecí Stolec, Lake Lipno, Mount Horní Planá, and the hills in the east, we ate a hearty meal in the camp, enough to sustain us for our dangerous hike.

Pavel drilled us as we ate. Then he checked our outfits, tied the backpack straps, and made sure the caps were secured under our chins and the gloves tied to our sleeves. He slid his finger across razor-sharp knives, checked our revolvers, and ensured we had extra supplies of ammunition. Each of us also had a piece of dry smoked meat and some dried prunes in his breast pocket.

We were then introduced to our guide, a mysterious, tough-looking man who was about six feet tall. He looked like a nomad, with half of his face hidden behind a scarf. He had been scrutinizing us from a few yards off; he did not know us, but his job was to lead us from the encampment westward on the mountain trail before dark.

At 4:00 p.m. our guide signaled to us to move out. We embraced Pavel, and then followed our strange-looking leader.

We followed the mountain trail for about an hour and a half. Between the steep cliff walls our steps echoed like drumbeats, so we walked cautiously. At about 5:30 p.m. we turned south. The guide stopped, listened for sounds, and gave us brief instructions.

"At all costs," he said quietly to us, pointing to a group of hills that seemed to slowly fall in the penumbra of the sunset, "you must avoid the valley path by at least four hundred meters. The Communist National Safety Federation (CNSF) patrols there with their dogs all the time."

As the guide checked our outfits and weapons, his scarf accidentally slipped from his face, exposing a grotesquely scarred cheek. He noticed my shock and mumbled, "You've got to watch out for the damned dogs, or they will tear you apart." With that, he vanished into the bush between the rocks and was gone.

From where we parted from our guide, we would be in hazardous terrain and on our own for about fifteen hours before reaching the border. Each of us knew the way from the detailed instructions we received earlier, which used the peaks of the mountains as directional landmarks.

Still, without the guide, we were frightened, and for the first time felt the heavy burden of being lost in the wilderness. The vision of the guide's mauled face and the fear of being without him lingered. The sun fell behind the cliffs, and darkness cloaked us. Our future seemed as mysterious as the deepening gloom of the eastern horizon.

"We'll wait for the moon," I said.

Cold winds blasted light snow in our faces, but despite our discomfort we wished for even more of it; the CNSF patrolled less during storms, as snow-disoriented dogs were useless.

Soon a thin layer of powder covered the ground and the moon illuminated the steep path. The snow protected us from the dogs, but it slowed our advance on the slippery rocks. It was tough going. Sweat dripped from our brows and mixed with the melted snow; in spite of a temperature drop, we all felt the heat of our physical exertion.

At about midnight, Mirek motioned that we should stop to eat and rest. We could pause for only a few minutes, for we had to reach the other side of the mountain while the moon still lit our way. We felt clumsy as we climbed over the slick rocks and thought about the patrols' killer dogs, which could sniff out anyone within a five hundred-meter radius if the wind blew in the right direction.

Patrols might have been anywhere in our path. Although the guards stayed mostly on the trails, sometimes they hid in the bush, letting escapees approach them accidentally. The dogs were trained to be silent and act only upon command; then the guards would make an easy arrest.

After a few minutes or so we moved on, dragging ourselves down the slope at around 5:00 a.m.; it was still dark. At the bottom we all collapsed in an exhausted heap. Although the sunrise was still hours away, the terrain became visible from the sun's reflection behind the horizon. After a short rest we crossed the saddle and climbed up the wooded hill, staying away from the valley path the guide had warned us to avoid.

From the summit we saw a cold, black maze of more hills in the distance. Dense fog filled the winding valleys. I feigned courage to strengthen my companions, pretending that the remaining two or three kilometers would be the easy part of the journey; in my heart I doubted this was true.

Another slippery descent made us aware that the escape was far from complete. We crawled on until daybreak, when we reached the bottom close to 8:00 a.m. There, we could confidently rest for an hour or so. From there we walked up the last small hill, behind which lay five hundred meters of open fields that led to freedom.

As we gathered ourselves together again and began to walk up the last slope, we heard a distant howl, and then one closer. We froze.

"They won't get me," I thought, and shouted aloud to my companions, "Let's get to that high ground! There we can fight the beasts!"

We scrambled up the hill, gaining the plateau as six huge German shepherds advanced upon us. We opened fire and shot five of the dogs, but the sixth evaded a spray of bullets. The guide's face seemed to flash before me when the dog charged, choosing me as his target. I dropped my empty revolver and pulled out my knife. The dog leapt, straining for my throat, but as it did I disemboweled it with a single stroke. As it fell it crushed me to the ground, covering me with its foul guts.

The dogs were followed by the guards, discharging their rifles. Tonda and Lojza were killed instantly, but Mirek and I managed to reload and return their fire. The guards retreated, hiding behind trees about one hundred meters from our plateau, which gave us time to empty the pockets of Tonda and Lojza of anything that would even remotely identify them, or any of us, or Pavel's camp.

It occurred to me that the guards were as frightened as we were. The uphill distance to the elevated plain gave us an advantage, and with a burst of adrenaline, Mirek and I raced across the open field and then collapsed, not knowing whether we actually made it across the German border. We were found minutes later by the Bavarian patrol; they had heard all the shots and came to investigate. When we revived, a patrolman drove us to the village of Freyung, and at the Grenzpolizei station we were given first aid and food. I asked the officers to notify the Regensburg Civil Intelligence about our arrival; that afternoon, on November 13, 1948, we were in protective custody in the Freyung jail. Before I fell asleep later that evening, I couldn't stop reviewing the scene on the hilltop. Good God! All four of us were so damned close!

This thought kept me awake as I tried to sort out what was happening. Today we had been helped by the Germans, who were our enemies during World War II; they had helped us to escape from our "liberators"! I knew I had much to learn in order to understand these confusing issues.

Never before had I crossed a border as we did today. The crossing was only half successful; we lost two friends, and we didn't know how Mirek and I would end up. We would long remember the violent moments we experienced as we said good-bye to Bohemia, killing six fierce dogs, and, perhaps, also injuring the guards. I would have a hard time reconciling some of this, and already I felt no pride in the things I had been forced to do to survive. It was called self-preservation, yet the fear of what was left behind and of what was ahead hung over me like a shroud stained with despair, warning me that this was all just the beginning. Was I ready for it?

◄ *Charles Novacek was*
named Karel (Czech
for Charles) after his
grandfather Karel
(left) and uncle Karel
(center); Seated right is
Františka Nováčková,
Charles' grandmother.

▼ *Maria and Antonin*
Nováček , 1922.

▷ Charles Novacek's birthplace and home in Ožďany, Slovakia.

◁ Charles Novacek next to one of his father's beehives, 1930.

◁ Charles Novacek,
1937.

▲ Vlasta and Charles
Novacek, 1932.

◁ Charles Novacek with
his first .22 caliber rifle,
1933.

147

△ *Charles and Vlasta
Novacek.*

▷ *Vlasta and Charles
Novacek.*

⊲ *Charles Novacek,*
1932.

⌃ *Charles Novacek,*
1937.

⊲ *Charles Novacek,*
1934.

▷ *Nováček family and friends in the Tatra Mountains, 1932.*

▲ *Nováček family camping near Brusno, 1933.*

▷ *Nováček family portrait.*

< Charles' friend Etelka.

^ Charles' friend Sylva.

^ Charles Novacek, 1940.

▷ *Tank on Náměšt' nad
Oslavou town square,
1945.*

▾ *Charles Novacek's
student identification
for State School of
Industrial Engineering,
Brno, 1948.*

◄ *Charles Novacek.*

▾ *Charles Novacek at work for the Augsburg Resettlement Center.*

153

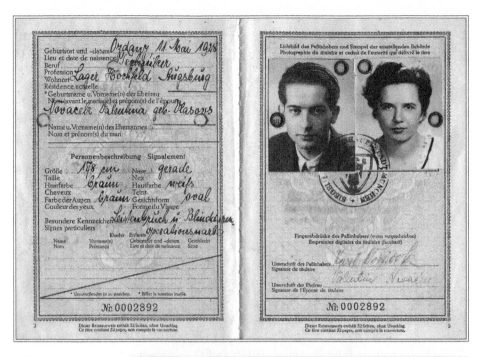

> ⌃ *Charles and Valentina Novacek, documents for travel to Venezuela, 1951.*

> ⊳ *Charles and Sandra Novacek at an art show opening, 1997.*

◁ *Charles Novacek*
in front of a plaque
honoring Josef Robotká
for his work in the
Czech Resistance,
Velká Bíteš, 1997.

⌄ *Self-portrait of*
Charles Novacek
overlooking downtown
Detroit, Michigan, 1996.

six

DISPLACED PERSONS CAMP

I lived my sad youth until freedom came,
When everyone breathed a sigh of relief
And I believed I could start a new and happier life.
Now I work with joy and try to prove that
I am an effective member of the human race.

LECHFELD

EARLY THE NEXT morning we two Czech refugees climbed into a Freyung police car heading west to Regensburg. The driver dropped Mirek at the Regensburg Refugee Center, and me just a few blocks farther along, at the United States Counter Intelligence Corps (CIC) for debriefing.

Captain Kochinski inspected and personally cross-examined me. Classified data from the Bohemian underground authenticated me, and after a short review of the documentation, the captain introduced me to his superior, Major Warren. In German, I presented Pavel Kominek's proposal: that in exchange for intelligence, the Americans would support our resistance. However, Warren confirmed that the Americans were not permitted direct involvement; therefore, they refused us.

Still, they wanted an uninterrupted supply of intelligence, and for that they offered money. Pavel specifically instructed me to reject any such arrangements. Our discussions continued for an additional day, but in the end no agreement was reached. Our meeting was interrupted by a report from Bohemia. In a massive raid near Vimperk, 159 people, including Pavel Kominek, had been killed, and hundreds more arrested. The raid reduced the ranks of our Czech Resistance group drastically, and I thus became virtually useless to the Americans, having lost so many contacts at home. All of our talks ended, and I was registered in the International Refugee Organization (IRO) camp. The Americans found mercenaries to fill their need for information, and in all likelihood I was to be forgotten.

When I arrived in the IRO collection center, Mirek had already received his displaced persons identification. He showed me some short-cuts and how to get daily rations without standing in a long line. We slept in one room with eighteen other men. We never talked about the border crossing with the other camp inmates.

Mirek and I reached Bavaria in time to see the unresolved consequences of the Second World War and the beginning of the new Cold War. Our homeland was torn by unrest, and Germany was flooded with an overpopulation of refugees. Like our own, many other nations became satellites held close to the Soviet Union by the Iron Curtain, which stretched from Berlin to the Black Sea. We had seen the invasion of Czechoslovakia, Poland, Hungary, and Yugoslavia in 1945, and how these territories had become like a bomb threatening to explode.

IRO authorities moved us from camp to camp until February 25, 1949, when, shortly before midnight, an unheated bus from the Würzburg collection center slowed at the Displaced Persons (DP) Camp Lechfeld and unloaded forty-two men, women, and children, including

Mirek and me. The camp had been a small air base for the German armed forces; it had been destroyed as a base near the war's end. We were told it was the best place for people who were to stay a long time.

"God forbid," I whispered, holding onto my empty stomach as we approached the frigid dining hall. One whiff of the foul air dispelled my hopes of a decent meal. Women and children had milk with their meager porridge; men had mere porridge. Camp officials gave each person two wool blankets, one field cot, and one cot straw sack. Families and women were escorted to a heated barracks adjacent to the kitchen, and we six single men were sent to air terminal Room 25, at the edge of a demolished runway; nearby, several unusable demolished buildings formed a part of the encampment. The air terminal itself had no electricity, and the darkness hid the other missing necessities. Windows lacked glass; in fact, Room 25 didn't even have a window frame. Ironically, the room number attached above the door was spotless, though so much else was decrepit or filthy.

To keep out the cold, Mirek and I fastened two blankets over the opening. Four other men unclasped the field cots, shored up the door, and shifted the cots together so we could keep warm. On the following morning, we all found straw to stuff the cot sacks. Mirek located tarpaper for the window and I dug up an old air duct in a burned-out building. Our first full day at Camp Lechfeld ended warmer for the six of us in Room 25, but the one bowl of porridge daily failed to fill our empty bellies.

Camp Lechfeld opened in 1948 exclusively for Czech refugees. I learned, through my observations and some discreet inquiries, that other nationals occupied better-organized camps; because these had opened in 1945, the occupants had had more time to improve them, while mediocre administrators provided the new refugees with only the bare necessities. Just a half a kilometer away from the Czech camp was a well-maintained Jewish camp that housed 200 families. I wandered around there a few times until a guard ordered me out; we were not allowed there. Unfortunately, Camp Lechfeld was run by corrupt officials appointed by the IRO, who robbed the camp of its allocated stock and sold it to German farmers. I discovered that much-needed supplies were not reaching the camp; I also learned that these racketeers guarded their "loot" well. For fear of my own safety I stopped my investigations.

Resettlement of displaced persons went according to the yearly quotas for each country; therefore, the entry date to a DP camp was important for refugees. That date determined when someone would have the right to emigrate. Mirek and I would be eligible in two years. Employment and residency outside the camp made the date void. If a refugee found a job outside a camp, he or she would have to make other emigration arrangements.

Mirek and I tried, but found no way out. Others who tried living outside the camp returned or were brought back, having been arrested by the police for loitering.

The camp authorities relocated us from Room 25 to a larger room, Room 244, and increased the number of occupants to forty-eight. They arranged two rows of bunks in three levels, without space in between; the top bunk only had room to stretch, not to sit up. The room was dark, except for the wan light that snuck in through the boarded windows during the day.

Our rations diminished. Toilets and washing facilities froze, and we all became infested with vermin and disease. I couldn't believe so many lice could exist in one armpit; with my hand I scraped out layers of them, soaked with blood. Our starving, idle bodies grew foul. The camp "medicine man" came daily to pump DDT powder into our beds, under our arms, between our legs, and into the air; despite this, countless lice were already deeply embedded in our skin.

Such was the situation in Room 244.

My own condition deteriorated. Since death from starvation and disease seemed imminent, I crawled to an infirmary of the nearby Jewish camp to beg for help. Avoiding the guard, I crept under the barbed wire fence and found a trap door in the back of the infirmary. That door led me to a lovely and humane nurse, who took me in. She applied a thick black paste over the skin where the lice were already deeply rooted. After a few hours, she washed away layers of dead bugs. A hot bath and clean ragged clothing, boiled by the nurse, changed me back to a human being again. She even gave me some food, and then let me back out through the trap door so the guard would not see me. The opening in the barbed wire fence, covered with rubbish, lay behind a half-destroyed barn next to the infirmary. I crawled under the fence, replaced the trash, and looked back to see the nurse's face at the window. It was the face of an angel.

I was not far from where my roommates lay, but I could not yet return to the air terminal building. In one of the destroyed buildings nearby, I cleaned a space in the attic and stayed there alone for a few days. The spring rains forced the earthworms out, and they provided me with just enough protein to survive; washed well and boiled in my meal dish, they were not half bad.

I went back for Mirek, who lay with the others in that infested room, and dragged him over to meet my Jewish nurse so he could also be freed of lice. I cleared a space for him in my attic and fed him with worms. The camp kitchen still doled out porridge once a day. Slowly, we gained a little strength.

We decided one day to walk twenty-two kilometers to the Augsburg IRO Resettlement Center hoping to find help. The hike for two men as weak as we were was long and painful, but we were rewarded for our efforts; near the center's kitchen we found a waste dump of food, and that meant survival. The center cook spotted us rifling through the garbage, and out of pity he gave us a huge bowl of hot cabbage soup and fresh bread.

A sweat broke out under my eyes as I ate; the soup dish rattled in my trembling hands. Each swallow made my mouth water; it passed over my taste buds and slipped gently into my stomach. I almost burned with joy; I ate very, very slowly. I wanted the soup to last a long time. I would remember that moment later, almost every time I ate soup—especially if it was a cabbage soup.

After we finished the soup, the cook gave us two burlap sacks, which we filled with the old wasted loaves of bread from the food dump, and then we returned to Lechfeld to feed the other forty-six men in Room 244. Seeing the sacks of bread, they all were revived. From then on, the men daily walked the distance to the dump to collect sacks of stale food.

As the months passed and spring progressed, the thaws came and we finally had water again. Men cleaned the room, debugged it with some of the black paste the nurse had given me, washed themselves, boiled their clothing, shaved, cut their hair, and continued to walk to Augsburg for stale, but welcome food. I stopped eating worms.

In summer, though, the hunger returned anew because the food was spoiled in the heat; however, Mirek and I were not there to witness it because we received a three-month reprieve, from June through August.

Our American friends, Captain Kochinski and Major Warren, called us to join an American training camp near Rothenburg. We trained for those three months for action behind the enemy lines in Israel. According to the United Nations plan of 1947, the Jewish State was established in 1948, dividing Palestine into Arab and Jewish states, respectively. Israel had about 7,990 square miles and approximately 4.2 million inhabitants; Jerusalem was the capital. We were enthusiastic about the prospect of being useful and helpful; plus, we were well fed and clothed, and the training was remarkably stimulating. I did very well with it, and was among those with the highest ratings; my gymnastics, skiing, horseback riding, and tennis activities paid off. Our last task in the training was to jump out of an airplane. In this I failed miserably; the sergeant had to kick me out; otherwise I would not have been allowed to participate in the campaign in Israel. However, the planned engagement in Israel was cancelled and the training camp was disbanded; I never found out exactly why.

Mirek and I were shipped back to Lechfeld. What I did not know was that before we left the training camp, Mirek had managed to conceal a service revolver with some ammunition; he told me about it after we arrived in Lechfeld again.

Food shortages made the men in Room 244 vulnerable and weak again. Many had enlisted in the French Foreign Legion, whose agents shamelessly recruited men from DP camps. In all, twenty-eight men from our room had enlisted with the Legion. Mirek and I once waited where the "Légion étrangère" bus usually parked; that particular day the bus did not appear. I felt it might be a sign, and we did not go there again. Years later I learned that all but one of the men had perished in the Far East.

Those remaining told us how bad it had become in July, when the food from the Augsburg dump spoiled in the heat. Mirek and I started to feel ill within a few days of our return, since we could not feed ourselves in the manner to which we had become accustomed in the training camp.

One day, when it was my turn to go to Augsburg for food, I spoke to the cook who had given me soup a few months before; he was glad to see me again. I told him about our dilemma; he promised to save what he could and give it to us in a bag, though he was not truly allowed to do so.

I now had better clothing, so I walked to the offices of the IRO and asked about work. Already discouraged and feeling out of place in offices that I knew nothing about, I felt as if I should just walk back to pick up the bread bag and return to Lechfeld to feed the hungry; but then a heavily accented voice called to me, and a man explained that in Lager Hochfeld, a group of apartment houses across the way, was a sewing shop, and the foreman of the shop was looking for somebody to maintain and repair the sewing machines. I thanked him and headed straight for the subdivision of old buildings to ask the way. It was in the last building, and stood about a kilometer from the resettlement center.

The two-story building, about three hundred feet long, housed two floors of sewing machines and a large storage room. As I entered, I found I did not understand a word the women sewers were speaking; to me, it was a mixture of gibberish and the hum of the Singer machines. I soon found out that all the women were from the Baltic states—Estonia, Latvia, and Lithuania. I also learned that German was universal, and I could communicate with everyone using this language. They told me that a Mr. Kivi was in charge of the shop, and one of them showed me to his office.

It turned out that Mr. Kivi had a major problem; he was managing a sewing shop of about eighty seamstresses, eight large tables with cutters, several fitters and designers, not to mention frequent large deliveries of new fabric. Used clothing coming from steam cleaners for refabrication comprised the greatest volume of deliveries. The problem was that Mr. Kivi knew nothing about sewing new or repairing used clothing, and knew even less about maintaining the machines. Two Estonian fellows took care of more than eighty machines, but having been injured in the war, each of them had only one arm. Most of the seamstresses were women who had never done such a job professionally; in Europe women usually sewed as part of their household duties. I could not judge the cutters; however, as Mr. Kivi was explaining that the sewing machines needed more attention, I observed that incompetent seamstresses were inadvertently abusing the machines.

At that point I wasn't too sure I wanted the job. Perhaps Mr. Kivi noticed my hesitation, because he then said that although the pay was not too high, a room with access to a kitchen came with it. He was also quick to add that there was another room a block and a half from there in a building where other Czechs lived. I was confused, but fear of Room 244 in Lechfeld made me decide quickly; I told Mr. Kivi I would be back in a few days and to hold it for me. It was settled.

I walked to Lechfeld with the bag of bread and told Mirek what I had done. He was glad, and thought that by being closer to the Resettlement Center in Augsburg, we might have a better chance of securing emigration and escaping from the hellhole we were in altogether.

That day was a Friday, and we decided to start on the following Monday. We did not expect difficulties with the camp leader, because we would just transfer from one camp to another. We lay there, thinking of the new chapter that might be about to open, and I soon noticed that Mirek had fallen asleep.

A board had been removed from the window to let some air into the room; I looked through it and was reminded of how it was at home. I hummed a tune I used to sing at the Oasa Cabaret in Brno.

Suddenly, the door opened and a stranger walked in. He addressed me with a pleasant voice and introduced himself as Mr. Rybnišek from Brno; what a coincidence! He told me he had been looking for me, and that the camp leader told him he would find me there. An animated conversation ensued as he started to speak about familiar people and places. I was very happy to hear about my hometown. After a little while, he suggested we go out for a short walk, as the shade in the nearby forest would be more pleasant than the close air of Room 244. We did so, slowly heading to the river Lech; not crossing the airfield, but going through the woods. I was so enthralled by hearing all of the news from home that I did not realize until we were already in the forest that I neglected to waken Mirek so he could also come along and hear it.

Unexpectedly, I saw Mirek out of the corner of my eye, hiding near the building, looking in our direction. I thought it was odd, but I thought nothing much of it. Once he was out of sight in a moment, he was also out of mind.

The river was another mile or so away, and as we walked toward it I fully devoted my attention to Mr. Rybnišek, who continued to tell me all about my country. His voice was soft, and hearing the Czech language was so wonderful.

We were approaching the rocks, and just beyond them the Lech River flowed. I asked Rybnišek how he found me and what his connection to our resistance was, because he knew details about both my family and Pavel Kominek. His answer to my questions was to walk several steps ahead of me, turn, and pull out a revolver; but before I could even move or shout out, or before he could shoot me, Mirek shot his hand. Though we were in shock, we overpowered him; then we tied him up and I ran to the camp leader's office to call the CIC headquarters in Regensburg while Mirek made sure our prize did not escape.

I told Captain Kochinsky what happened. He at once called the CIC office in Augsburg, and within an hour they came and had Rybnišek in custody. He was taken to Landsberg, where he was identified as a

Czech-Communist hit man who had killed at least one American agent. He was tried, sentenced, and executed.

I had literally and figuratively dodged a bullet, thanks to Mirek.

Needless to say, I returned to Mr. Kivi a few days later than I promised, but luckily the job was still available. He assigned me a room on the second floor in the building, where several Czechs were already living. To get better acquainted with the shop, Mr. Kivi paired me for work with a young Estonian in the storeroom; her name was Magda, and she was married and had a young son. Her husband was being held by the Soviet Army as a POW. It wasn't known when he would be released; many POWs never showed up. I liked working with Magda; it was a quiet, seemingly safe environment, and my sense of masculinity, much damaged in prison, began to recover somewhat in her presence. Part of me longed to test the waters, but it did not seem to be an honorable thing to do and nothing ever came of it.

Because our building was close to the Resettlement Center, Mirek could investigate emigration possibilities and keep me informed. The Czechs who lived with me were all students and professionals, and in one of the rooms resided Dr. Landa, a lawyer in charge of the Augsburg Resettlement Center's legal department. It thus turned out that I did not work for Mr. Kivi too long, because I soon got another job as a legal clerk for Dr. Landa. In November of 1949, I was promoted to a chief clerk with a substantial increase in salary. After a few weeks in the legal office, I exposed the improprieties of Camp Lechfeld to higher IRO officials. The camp leader and his cohorts were arrested and punished.

The occupants of Camp Lechfeld were moved to better camps or emigrated to new homes in other lands. They carried with them their nightmares, and they carried with them a host of physical and psychological woes. Most likely, they would never rid themselves of cancer risk, chronic colitis, ulcers, arthritis, mental disorders, and insomnia. Perhaps the DDT powder remained embedded in their systems; maybe their experiences of loss and deprivation left them scarred. For me personally, the worst immediate ailment was colitis from all the awful food. Much later in my life I would experience insomnia, depression, and anxiety as a result of my misfortunes.

The new German military, under the United States' auspices, built a new base in Lechfeld. New buildings, roads, and runways completely changed the appearance of the place, covering the face of the dismal past forever. The life of DPs improved in most camps, but the Cold War between the East and West intensified. The Berlin airlift ended when the Soviets lifted the blockade, but their constant threat to the Western powers never stopped. It seemed that the Soviet satellites, such as Czechoslovakia, were cut off from Western civilization forever.

We found ourselves at Camp Hochfeld, which was very different from Camp Lechfeld. Hochfeld had been a large subdivision of apartment buildings for German military personnel. In 1945, the subdivision became a displaced persons camp exclusively for refugees from the Baltic States. The apartments were all two- or three-bedroom units with kitchens and bathrooms. Families were assigned rooms, and even single persons could room one, two, or three together; the kitchen was common for all.

Nearby was a large military base and barracks. It had been reorganized, and after 1945 was used by the IRO as a resettlement center and emigration office. The facilities there included offices of embassies, consuls, medical screening offices, legal offices, and security. In the large buildings and barracks were housed emigrants in transit, and the adjacent kitchen—where Mirek and I found leftover food for the hungry in

Lechfeld—fed both the employees and the emigrants. Most employees of the IRO were residents of Camp Hochfeld, which had a sizable sewing shop, a large open barracks for occasional entertainment, and storage buildings for used clothing for refugees and food supplies for the camp residents.

Mirek and I lived on the second floor in Block 12 with other Czechs who were also employees of IRO. Mirek was accepted within a couple of weeks by the Australian consul and emigrated there soon thereafter. I wanted to go to the United States, and waited to go through an extensive screening process. While waiting, I worked for Dr. Landa. When Mirek left for Australia, I became lonely, so I arranged for activities after work to keep myself fit both physically and mentally.

Close by was a fine riding school owned by Herr Pfan, an old Vienna Derby jockey and also a graduate of the Imperial Vienna Riding School. To get acquainted, I took classes from him and discovered that besides being an excellent horseman, he spoke Hungarian, giving me the opportunity to practice the language instead of merely translating Hungarian documents at the office for emigrants in transit. Since I was also a good horseman, we became friends and he suggested I give lessons to some of his students; for this, he would give me lessons in the kind of horsemanship used by the Imperial Vienna Riding School. It was a fine arrangement. A tailor made me riding pants and a jacket, and the shoemaker made me a pair of riding boots; I began to look like a real horseman.

Herr Pfan also introduced me to the Augsburg Fencing Club, where I practiced twice a week under the supervision of a skilled fencing master. The club sold me a fencing uniform, and soon I was mixing with the Bavarians who admired me for daring to join them despite the international turmoil. After all, to them I was a foreigner; but since I spoke German well the locals accepted me with open arms.

The second week in December 1949, the IRO manager asked me to go for a week to the Munich Resettlement Center to help with translations from Russian into German for several Russian families; they lived in a nearby settlement and needed to file their documents for processing so they could emigrate. They already had a German-to-English translator; I did not know a word of English then, so translations had to be made from Russian to German to English. I made some good friends among the old Russian emigrants, and several older ladies smothered me with kindness.

I returned to Hochfeld before Christmas and continued my work in the legal office. The IRO manager complimented me for the translations I did in Munich. I was paid as usual and my transport and food were free. I also resumed lessons at the riding school, and I was assigned another student: Miss Vlasov. She actually did not need that much teaching, for she was already a fairly good horsewoman herself. She lived with her parents and a younger brother on the second floor of a building across the street from the sewing shop in Hochfeld.

Before the holidays there was a Christmas party in the barracks. A small group of Czech musicians played the latest dance selections, and I was their part-time crooner and sang one tune in each language I knew: Czech, Slovakian, Hungarian, Russian, and German.

I also danced a tango and a waltz with Miss Vlasov. "*No nichevo,*" she said, explaining to me later, when we became closer, how the expression was to be understood: *Not too bad!* The tone of voice she used suggested something more than mere approval of my singing or dancing. In an instant, I felt myself finally recovering from the trauma inflicted on my masculinity by the torture of the prison guards; Miss Vlasov's soft voice whispering innuendos convinced me there might yet be life after prison for this man.

She then told me she had heard about me from the old Russian emigrants in Munich; what they told her made her curious, and she took a few days off from the classes she attended at Munich University's medical school to investigate.

So began something fresh and new in my life.

DP CAMP HOCHFELD

In truth, Miss Vlasov—actually, now Doctor Vlasov—did not take off from classes just because of me; she finished her studies and was now waiting for her official graduation and diploma. Her family planned to emigrate to the United States, and she hoped to go with them.

Her parents and brother Eugene left by rail transport to the ship anchored near Genoa, in the Mediterranean, on December 28, 1949. Valentina did not travel with them.

When the riding lessons at Herr Pfan's stables resumed, I saw Valentina every other day. We grew closer as she told me the story of her family from Rēzekne, Latvia. The German occupation began in 1940 and ended in 1944 with the Soviet offensive; but just as in Czechoslovakia, the liberators turned out to be as bad as the Germans. I already knew how the Soviet satellites all over Europe and Asia had suffered under Soviet rule; Valentina's story enlightened me in detail about the tragic years of the Baltics.

The escape of the Vlasov family from Rēzekne had been truly remarkable. They were not involved in any resistance activities; nor did they associate with dissidents rebelling against the Soviets. Just because Mr. Vlasov was a landowner, the Communists had listed him and his family for deportation to Siberia. A friend warned him about it, so he was able to save them from certain destruction. Their flight from Latvia to Western Europe took them many weeks, and several times they were separated from one another due to disorder and complications with railroad connections. Finally, in 1944, they were reunited near Augsburg and survived as farm workers until Camp Hochfeld was established in 1945 by the American IRO.

Mr. Vlasov was a builder-developer and was skilled in many fields; so whatever trade was needed, he could support his family well. Mrs. Vlasov was a talented seamstress and knew how to maintain a household in even the most difficult times. Their son started high school, and Valentina entered the Munich University system, pursuing a career in dentistry. However, Mr. Vlasov became seriously ill, and in 1949 was diagnosed with terminal stomach cancer. By then, Valentina was close to finishing school and was able to make important contacts in the Augsburg hospital, so her father would get better attention. The family was scheduled to emigrate at the end of the year, and a bad prognosis would prevent the whole family from doing so. The emigration officers were very strict about this; Mr. Vlasov's misfortune would have destroyed them all. His doctors showed mercy on him, and on his family; the hospital records were rewritten in a format to allow Mr. Vlasov and his family to emigrate.

On July 19, 1950, Valentina and I decided to marry. We were compelled by our extreme loneliness, and our engagement gave us a reason to join forces against the world. Learning how to love under the very worst circumstances bonded our lives together and sharpened the need we developed for each other. We came from different little corners of the world with different religions, languages, customs, and education; but we both wished dearly for freedom.

My Estonian friends helped me to get a suitable room, so Valentina and I could live together. It faced the main street, and we shared a kitchen with another couple, Mr. and Mrs. Neuberger; they were Hungarians, fifteen years older, excellent bridge players, well educated and well read. They became pleasant companions for us. Mrs. Neuberger cooked fine meals that we shared with them for a reasonable contribution; this was important for me, since the colitis I had developed in Camp Lechfeld became a serious impediment in my daily activities, and I had to hide it from the IRO emigration officers.

I introduced Valentina to Mr. Karl Stritesky, my fencing master at the Augsburg Fencing Club. We both took instructions from him during our stay in Augsburg. So busy with horses and fencing, our waiting time for emigration seemed to go by more smoothly.

With Valentina's help, I translated documents not just into German, but also into English from many languages, and was thus able to make some more money. We had little experience with how to make life bearable in such distasteful settings, but we learned quickly; we tried to maintain good physical and mental health, to stay out of trouble, to earn money to afford better food, and to see, if possible, an occasional movie, opera, or concert. This relatively peaceful existence was sometimes disturbed by requests from IRO emigration officers for additional information for our documents, calls from the medical examiners for further x-rays or tests, and more questions from the consul. We were thoroughly screened for any issues or defects; often I thought that citizens of the United States had to be superior to us.

My father was on my mind a great deal. I knew I had been violating his rule about women and honor, so I moved to do something about it; Valentina and I set October 26, 1950, as our wedding day. Our friends in the apartment and Herr Pfan, our riding teacher, were happy to hear of it; Herr Pfan even offered his horses to carry all four of us—that is, the witnesses and us—to downtown Augsburg to the registrar's office as in the old days. I was excited about the prospect of marrying in one of the most historically celebrated cities in Europe; the horses tied in front of the old *Standesamt* would sound a chord of tradition.

However, as the twenty-sixth approached, we changed our plans and married on the twenty-fifth instead. We were concerned about unnecessary publicity, which could possibly harm our relations with the IRO authorities; for us, favorable interactions with them were most important. Unexpected problems arose anyway; we were informed we would now have to reapply for emigration, because Valentina's name and my single status had changed. We reapplied as soon as we found out about it, but almost a year later the United States authorities continued to drag their feet on the processing. My goal to reach America met many obstacles, and I was tired of the bureaucratic demands; I became impatient. We had discovered Valentina was pregnant, and I did not want my child to be born in Germany; after the treatment I had gone through at the hands of the Nazis, I still retained abhorrence toward many things German.

We found out that the Venezuelan government was taking emigration applications. They invited us, and on July 1, 1951, we completed the paperwork. We went through the immigration procedures in Munich, took the train through the Alps to Italy, and landed in a second-class hotel in Genoa, where we prepared to sail westward.

GENOA

Three months in Genoa was too short a time to learn about the magnificent metropolis. I was humbled by the history, the cemetery carvings that illustrated the tradition of ordinary people's devotion to their ancestry in the afterlife, and the streets where the very old and the contemporary merged as if in one single tune and rose to eternal Heaven.

These streets were busy during the day, shifting notes from very loud to soft and then to loud again, as if composing songs for dancing from one curb to another. The cobblestone paving resonated with the impact of horses' hooves that echoed off the buildings and impressed bystanders. At sunset sentimental melodies invited one to nearby cafés. The red Chianti, rather inexpensive in Genoa, was my favorite wine, and the empty bottles were convenient objects to throw from the window at obnoxious cats wailing through the night. My sleep was erratic, filled with the residue of nightmares from prison and Camp Lechfeld. When we finally boarded the ship *Amerigo Vespucci* for an eleven-day sail to Caracas on October 24, 1951, I slept well at last.

We were scheduled to arrive in La Guaira, Venezuela—Caracas' harbor—on November 6. On the ship, Valentina's morning sickness increased. My "free ride" had ended, making me think of all the responsibilities that lay ahead.

seven

THE VENEZUELAN EXPERIENCE

I had not yet approached the New World.
What little I knew was gained from studies and travelers.
I knew of the United States, but knew far less of South
America.
Venezuela was a challenge for me,
yet much unexpected help came my way,
which motivated me to go beyond the mere headlines
of history.
I will never forget those remarkable people,
especially an illiterate native woman
who changed my wife and me into better people.

W E SAILED FOR eleven days from Genoa, Italy, to La Guaira, Venezuela. As we approached, the Avila Mountains that crowned Caracas appeared depressing; the mountain shadows seemed to cast the city in gloom. The customs official confiscated my Solingen shaving knives as dangerous weapons; this was my first encounter with corrupt officials in Venezuela, for I figured he kept the knives for himself. In the harbor we were picked up and driven to Caracas, a nauseating hour-and-a-half ride through curves and steep cliff overhangs; as bad as it was for me, it was worse still for poor Valentina, as pregnant as she was.

Once in Caracas, we were introduced to the moderate tropical heat, and new insects we had never seen before. I did not know a word of Spanish, I didn't have a dime to my name, and I felt like a fool. Valentina had at least taken some classes in Spanish back home in Bavaria, when she anticipated our new destination. Plus, here I was, almost a father, but I knew nothing about raising a family. I hoped Valentina would know what to do. As soon as we settled in our small apartment, Valentina went to the American Embassy and registered us as emigrants asking for entry into the United States. That explained immediately how she felt about South America.

The streets of Caracas appeared much the same as those of Munich or Augsburg; jobs were not staring me in the face. I did not even know how to find a job. I felt strange. My father could have been of help to me; I found that whenever I felt I was in trouble, I thought of him. I was free, but I was just as forlorn as when I had been in prison, not knowing the future. How would I feed my family?

On the second Friday in November, I was introduced to car collision repair and painting. Valentina had read an ad stating that Ford Motor Company needed an experienced car painter. She called, and I had an appointment with the manager the following Monday. I couldn't believe it; she had told them I was the most experienced car painter Germany had ever had. I worked all Saturday and Sunday in an acquaintance's garage, trying to learn the ropes, because I had a chance to get the job if I just knew how to do it.

I introduced myself at the office of Mr. Boss—his name was genuine and singularly appropriate—just as Valentina had described to me, and I was hired as the master painter in charge of the exhibit car department.

I lucked out, though; I didn't actually have to paint. I was just the fore-man, and for several weeks I got away with my scheme and was able to pick up some knowledge about the job just by observing my workers. I was paid well, so I guarded my job in any way I could. I felt guilty, though, in my dishonest enterprise, but priorities dictated that I give the performance of a lifetime.

Valentina sympathized, but encouraged me to hang on. She said, "Maybe you actually know how to do it, and you don't even need to be afraid."

It turned out I didn't have to wait long to find out. The very next day orders came from Mr. Boss that the late model recently sent to our shop must be painted by the master painter; the car was thought to be for the exhibit on Sabana Grande. The excited workers made me even more anxious; they didn't even play baseball as they usually did dur-ing their lunch break, instead choosing to get the car ready. I sat and smoked my last cigarette in the break room. I might as well have been preparing for my execution. They finished their part by about 3:00 p.m. and then I applied the primer of red oxide.

The spraying started on top. The workers would move the stool I stood on, so I could reach far enough. They were very accurate and attended to every detail properly, so I wouldn't be interrupted. I could feel the sharp gaze of Pedro, the young man who wanted my job, as he observed me from afar. Usually apprentices applied the primer; for me, however, the priming was good practice, and I was glad for it. Pedro appeared to notice this.

The next morning I finished with a dark blue shade. It was polished, and the car delivered later that afternoon. Mr. Boss was pleased, and the car, the only one I ever painted all by myself, was placed on the turntable of the Sabana Grande Exhibit Hall. It seemed nothing short of a miracle, as though some supernatural force had helped me to do it; I wasn't superstitious, but I couldn't come up with any other way to explain the wonder. I even received a promotion after this stunt, though I never did fool Pedro.

With a trace of jealousy tingeing his voice, he said, "I'm glad you made it."

I believed he meant it. He was very clever, however, adding as he laughed, "For a car painter, you sure have soft hands."

ISLA DE MARGARITA: "A SHOUT IN THE SEA"

In March, we received a telegram from the governor of Isla de Margarita, off the coast of mainland Venezuela. It was an offer for Valentina to serve as a dentist to three villages around Juan Griego. She was glad to accept it; but the very next day she went into labor—early. In half an hour she gave birth to our first child, a two-month premature daughter. We named her Margarita, for she was supposed to have been born on Isla de Margarita. She had to be placed in an incubator, and Valentina stayed by her side. I accepted Valentina's assignment on her behalf, going to see the governor once Valentina and Margarita were cared for and resting. After a short interview, His Excellency the Governor Narvaez sent me to Dr. Rivas, the Director of the Ministry of Health, to receive the keys for the three clinics. He then introduced me to the custodian, Señorita Esbilia Mercedes Mata. Esbilia was about twenty-two, very thin, and apparently permanently and deeply bronzed by the sun. The cheekbones under her black eyes protruded sharply from her lean face; her mouth, always smiling, sparkled white. She had a fine aquiline nose, shiny black, long straight hair, and strong limbs. Here was someone who possessed Native American blood, at least in part.

She seemed polite, but I could not understand a word she said. Her fast-popping accent sounded preposterous to my ears—like a motorcycle. As best as I could, I asked her to slow down her speech, and found out she was one of the dental assistants assigned to Valentina in the Juan Griego district.

Esbilia was very helpful. In spite of my difficulty in understanding her, she helped me with everything. She found a house, an experienced maid, and some indispensable furnishings, like a kerosene refrigerator and stove and a water filter. She loaned me some pots and pans from her parents' house and also, most important, a mosquito net to install over our beds.

Setting up the barest necessities in my rented house, I checked out the produce market and then Esbilia showed me Valentina's clinic, the only one in Juan Griego reachable on foot; the other two were about four or five kilometers from our house. Esbilia explained that a taxi would drive Valentina there and back and would cost 50 bolivars per month for the service. Valentina's salary was 740 bolivars per month, and that would have to cover the cost of the taxi and three dental assistants, each 30 bolivars per month. That meant we ourselves would actually have 600 bolivars per month to work with. Our budget would be tight, but with the money I saved from the painting job, we would have a fair start.

Before returning to get my family, I made an agreement with the Ford dealer in Porlamar to purchase an old 1948 Plymouth for 600 bolivars, payable in twelve payments of 50 bolivars per month. Esbilia also showed me how to get to Porlamar by paying for a seat in a car, bus, or wagon, known as *carro por puesto*.

I returned to the mainland, picked up my family at Caracas Hospital, and we started immediately to pack. When I told Mr. Boss at

Ford Motor Company what was happening, he gave me a bonus of 100 bolivars and said he would have the job for me if I ever needed it again. He also wanted me to see Pedro, the would-be foreman, who now, rightfully, got the job. Pedro asked me, "Tell me the truth, Charles—what is your profession?"

When I confessed to him, he felt good about himself; he was proud he had helped a lost engineer. In a way, I felt sad to leave the painter's job—it paid 1,200 bolivars monthly—but I knew we had to start practicing our professions as soon as we could.

We had little to pack. From our one-room apartment we only had bed sheets and the two travel boxes from the DP camp in Germany. I wondered how I would conquer the country; the other *conquistadores* of old had started from Margarita and worked their way to the mainland, but I was doing it backward.

Since the conquest of Venezuela in 1499, many Europeans had come here to gain wealth. Some came, like we did, to establish a new home, since the Venezuelan government was kind enough to offer refugees a place to live. Like many South American nations, Venezuela wasn't involved in World War II; by helping refugees, however, they tried to even the score at least partially. Many refugees repaid the favor well and even became citizens; others found their utopia elsewhere.

For the moment we were settled in Isla de Margarita, "Pearl of the Caribbean," "A Shout in the Sea," "An Echo in the Village," as it was called in the commercials of the Radio Nuevo Esparta. Perhaps the "echo" was the cannon shot in 1498 from *La Pinta*, one of Columbus' caravels; on August 15, upon sighting the island, Columbus called it *Isla Santa*, or Holy Isle. I did not know, in the beginning, that the island would present a lasting fascination to me.

Ninety-two thousand natives and only twenty-six "imports" formed an unusual compendium of people, with diverse customs, behaviors, occupations, and ways of living. The only large-scale industry was fishing; otherwise, small farming, fruit, vegetable, and cattle production predominated. Paved roads did not exist. A few buses and jalopy taxis connected the outlying communities with the business center and the airport city Porlamar, which was situated on the south side of the island. Dr. Rivas directed all medical and dental services on behalf of the Ministry of Health from the Governor's office in La Asunción, the capital of the island. The road from Porlamar crossed the island north to our town of Juan Griego and led through La Asunción. The sixteen-mile drive took about an hour due to the bad roads, and some drivers could not make it through the Portachuelo Pass, which was little better than an animal trail that ran up and down steep hills in a saddle between two mountains. Sometimes the road washed away or filled with deep crevices, dangerous for any auto. I had to get used to them, because I would be driving on them.

The islanders were generous and devoutly Catholic, and each village had a church. While the schools were relatively primitive, like the dispensaries and hospitals, churches were rich and well maintained. In towns, some roads were paved and had shallow gutters. The conspicuous smell hinted of an absence of underground sewers and many surface trenches drained raw sewage. Still, the sidewalks were clean and free of trash; the storekeepers swept them daily, early in the morning. The grocery stores had some foodstuffs, but mostly sold alcoholic beverages and soda pop. Coca Cola signs were everywhere. The *Cerveza Caracas*—Caracas Beer—and soda pop was kept on ice at all times. People bought it and had a meal with a couple of bananas or *coro coro asado,* roasted fish *coro coro.*

Anyone could have a bar dispensing alcoholic beverages; one only needed a refrigerator, an ice maker, and a loud record player that blasted uncontrollably. It was hard getting used to the melancholic *rancheras* and the music of the mariachis; not because we did not like it, but because it was played at such a high volume. The songs actually reminded me of the Gypsy songs of my youth; in fact, I learned some of them and sang them one day on Radio Nueva Esparta, transmitted throughout the country.

Just a forty-foot-wide road separated our house from the beach. The waves from the north glazed the white sand, and the gulls and pelicans dove for fish close to the shore, even in the breaking surf. I dove there, like the pelicans, not for the fish, but to see marvels of nature new to me. Sometimes that surf was calm, and then the waves seemed motionless; here and there the water heaved and fell again. The bay looked like a mirror. In the spring the sea swelled; the ten-foot waves crashed over the sea wall, the road, and the two-foot high concrete curb in front of our house, though all these things had been built to stop them. East of our beach was an old ruined wooden dock, which was my special place. There I dove amid swarms of lobsters and other sea creatures that no doubt resented my intrusion, especially when I picked up one of them for a scrumptious dinner. The water was crystal clear, and in it, life prospered. A few yards away, where the bottom dropped deep, were treacherous shadows, demanding respect and cautious diving; even there, however, order, purity, and beauty prevailed.

I played with baby Margarita on this beach, and she swam by herself. She was just a few months old then, but she could hold herself afloat. The whole village came to see her; I threw her in the water, and she floated. The natives would moan and call me a *barbaro*—barbarian—but she was a natural.

I sometimes sat on the concrete curb in front of the house, in the skimpy shade of a crooked tree. I painted the sea and observed the fort on the hill across the bay. The Juan Griego fortress was built in the early sixteenth century for protection against pirates and adventurers; now only the ruins are visible, and a few old rusty cannons lay in the broken battlements. Legends claim Columbus anchored at a fair distance from the shore, sighted some Indians, and captured a few.

We ourselves did not capture any Indians; rather, they captured us, with their innocence and sincerity. They were delightful people. Esbilia came to visit frequently—to see if we needed anything. The house-keeper, Maria, kept our large colonial house, cooked, and attended to Margarita. Our home was an L-shaped, rather primitive structure, with a column-supported roof extending over a large concrete porch spanning the length of the house. The extended roof sloped into a large water tank. At first I didn't realize why it was so large; then I learned that during the rainy season it filled up, and the water then lasted a long time during droughts. The walls of the house framed the perimeter with untrimmed tree trunks as columns, connected with horizontal saplings and interwoven with bamboo lath; the roof was supported with raw, untrimmed rafters and also covered with bamboo lath. The lath, in both the roof and the walls, was plastered with mud containing straw reinforcement, mixed with prepared mortar or cement, and painted with lime. The roof valleys were lined with galvanized tin sheets, fastened with nails, and covered with bituminous paste, and the finished roof was covered with corrugated asbestos panels secured to rafters. A single surface-mounted cable through the house supplied lighting to each room; it was one of only a few houses in the area with electricity.

At the front of the house, between the water tank wall of the neighbor's house and the porch leading to our main entrance, was an open court. There, I made a playground for Margarita. In the center I sculpted a miniature fountain with a water jet fed from a large clay container placed on top of the water tank wall, which I filled manually. On the concrete wall I painted a mural representing my childhood vision of three pine trees on a hill—the father, the mother, and the child—mountains in the background, and a small cottage in the rolling country. My baby was safe in the playground; Maria always kept her eyes on her, because of the proximity of the sea and the lagoon. Also, though we had no snakes, we did have poisonous centipedes and scorpions hiding in the crevices of the houses.

I made many improvements to the house for us. I built a concrete water tank on the roof above the kitchen and purchased a pump to fill it with; there was sufficient water in the tank for everything, and we could even share it with neighbors. In the backyard I built a new shower and toilet—the only flushing toilet in town—with pipe leading into the salt lagoon; I used it as a sedimentation field and septic storage. From the tank above the kitchen, gravity's pressure on the water was sufficient for our shower and for filling the toilet tank for flushing; however, we couldn't flush too often, since we had to save water.

Soon we had two *chinchorros*, hammocks dangling from the columns for pleasant relaxation in the soft breeze from the sea. These were a gift from Esbilia; she and her mother made them to earn money, a craft that was a widespread cottage industry throughout the island. Esbilia and her parents were the most important contacts we had on the island. Their kindness came from the depth of their hearts, naturally; we never met anyone like them as we had drifted after war from place to place and found that most people seemed somewhat prejudiced against us.

By the time I met Valentina, the colitis I got from the infamous Camp Lechfeld improved; however, on the ship and in Caracas, with the change in drinking water, I became sensitive again. On the island it worsened further still, for drinking and cooking water had to be boiled for a minimum of seven minutes and filtered through stone elements, and not every source of food followed that dictum. Everything for consumption had to be washed with a solution made of boiled water and vinegar, and fruit and vegetables especially had to be carefully selected and washed with an even stronger solution. Diving, I harvested excellent sources of protein from the sea, but we didn't eat much beef at all, as it was too hard to chew. Pork we had sometimes, but we had fowl of various kinds more frequently. Regardless of what it was, it had to be carefully cleaned. Maria followed our cooking requirements, and when she prepared her own *coro coro asado*, roasted with garlic, she washed it carefully to our specifications before placing it over the open fire. It was a tasty and healthy delicacy we had often.

Valentina's reputation as a dentist rose quickly. Dr. Rivas assigned another three clinics to her and doubled her pay. Many people, including doctors from other communities and city officials, asked her to open a private office, like dentists on the other side of the island. The medical doctors living in the surrounding communities were foreigners and wanted to have their teeth attended to by a European dentist, but they would not go to the public dispensary, wanting to be cared for in private. We managed to put a private office together, borrowing money to do so; it was simple but useful and paid off.

The construction of a water dam was under way, and I became the assistant resident engineer under the supervision of an experienced civil engineer in charge of the whole project. I was a mechanical engineer, trained to design machines, but I soon found that engineering principles are applicable to all branches. With the help of my superior I quickly learned the things I needed to know in the science of soil mechanics.

Among other responsibilities assigned to me, the land survey of the projected area opened for me the whole spectrum of civil engineering. My change from mechanical to civil engineering became a necessity, because in Venezuela during those years there were few opportunities to practice mechanical engineering. In construction, however, jobs were abundant. Until the dam project was over in the spring of 1953, I worked and studied hard to place myself in line with other professionals; I had to be creative to meet unexpected challenges, and I had to become a civil engineer.

After the dam was completed on the island, I had no other opportunity to work there, so I sold the old Plymouth and went to Caracas to find a job. It turned out that Mr. Boss had left Venezuela, and I thus had no way to get back on Ford Motor Company's payroll. I lingered there for a few days and, feeling desperate, took a job as a common laborer for General Electric at 20 bolivars per day. It seemed like the difficult and monotonous job of a slave; I loaded and unloaded office furniture, and in a few short days I was more than sick of it. I couldn't understand why the Venezuelan government would go to Germany and recruit refugees, asking specifically for professionals, only to have no available employment for them. I grew disgusted with the whole thing, and decided to go to the top.

PRESIDENTIAL INTERVENTION

In June of 1953, I sent a telegram to the President of the Republic of Venezuela, which stated simply, "Your Excellency Marcos Pérez Jiménez, President of the Republic of Venezuela: Please grant me a short audience."

Given its brevity, it did not cost me too much to send it, and I did not expect anything to happen. I prepaid for two weeks for a room in the *Hostel la Pastora*, where I had lodging and food. I did not feel well; the food was wreaking havoc on my already delicate digestive system, and I was lonely for my family. I went out to shake off growing depression, only to meet up with an acquaintance who told me of the death of a colleague of Valentina's.

I did not need such news, as I was already saddened and anxious. I returned to my hostel, and when I did, there was a telegram from the President notifying me that he would see me. At this unexpected turn of events, I felt as if I were walking on water; still, at the same time, I was apprehensive, for I was unsure of how to handle myself. My clothing was rather shabby, I needed a haircut—which I could not afford—and my Spanish was less than fluent. It seemed almost better not to think of it.

Two days later I went to the capital, where I was ushered in to see His Excellency. He was sitting at his desk in all his grandeur, wearing a striking uniform. The expression on his face seemed rather pompous, and the glasses he wore made him appear too serious, rather gloomy and unattractive. In short, his countenance did not evoke in me any admiration or respect, but I nonetheless looked up to him because he was the president of a republic. He motioned for me to sit in the chair in front of him.

Oddly enough, I found that I understood him well. He asked who I was and what I wanted. Luckily, I had rehearsed my little speech several times, and it flowed from me quite smoothly. When I said I was from Czechoslovakia, he began to speak of the Czechoslovakian experiment in democracy, and that the Venezuelans wanted to use the United States constitution as a model, but it was too extensive; instead, they had used, at least in part, the Czechoslovakian one, and since that one had been itself based on the United States constitution, it came in handy.

I was amazed at how talkative he had become. Finally, after several minutes, I was able to tell him about my need for employment, and that having been invited by his government as an engineer, I expected there would be a job for me; I informed him that the opposite had proved true since my arrival. Although he was attentive, he said nothing specific or direct about my concerns and, after penning a short note, sent me to his secretary.

That was the end of my audience. I took the note, thanked him, stood up, and then, after bowing, followed his service man to another room. There, a middle-aged man was already writing another note, and it was addressed to Dr. Jesus Mijares, Ministry of Public Works, Director of Buildings. The man also explained to me how to get to Dr. Mijares' office, and said he would call him and tell him I was coming.

I was both excited and anxious about what I would find. When I arrived, the Director of Buildings encouraged me with his pleasant manner, and I felt even better about things when he sent me to meet the man who would be my future supervisor.

His name was Dr. Marcel Sous de Castro; he was about thirty-eight years old and a registered civil engineer. In Venezuela, all engineers were doctors, so I also became one; the only difference was that they all had money, while I had none.

That very day Marcel was awarded an inspection job for a large building, *Infanteria de Marina* (for the marine infantry) in Maiquetia, just north of the airport. It was a significant project and came to him with me attached. My salary was set at 1,200 bolivars per month. It all proved to be another exposure to the corruption inherent in Venezuela; I was hired because the person who awarded the contract specifically ordered that I be put on the payroll. I became the resident engineer responsible for the inspection of the project. Marcel didn't care about me being hired, for he was awarded a major contract with a sizable dividend attached.

I began to more completely understand how business in Venezuela worked. Later, when my professional efforts were recognized, Marcel became friendlier with me and let me in on many deals, to which I would not have otherwise been exposed. These deals ranged from being a little corrupt all the way to being very lucrative arrangements. I learned this was a standard operating procedure; in Venezuela, it was not considered dishonest. Although the standards did not seem straight or clear cut, I felt reasonably assured that in comparison to other immigrant families, mine would be safe.

Soon after I was hired, on a day on which I had just finished signing the weekly report for Marcel in my field office in Maiquetia, there was a commotion outside, and one of the workers yelled to me that there were soldiers coming with machine guns. I recognized the vehicle they accompanied as the presidential limousine. The car drove as close as it could to my field office on the hill; then His Excellency President Jiménez got out and walked toward me.

"How are you, Charles? How goes everything?"

I was extremely surprised and very pleased, because I never expected anything of the kind. It was exciting for me that President Jiménez was interested in my job; he wanted to see all the proceedings, and I was most ready to show him everything.

After we toured the building, he walked out, looking toward the north where low hills separated us from the sea. I said to him, "It seems strange to me, Your Excellency, that marines will not have entry to the sea. Here we are so close to it; yet there is no water."

"What are you saying?" he asked.

"We can cut this hill down in a few weeks and construct a wide boulevard to the sea. On the shore, a concrete dock can be made; a few rocks in the sea could be removed, and ships would have entry to the dock."

"Hmm," he said. "I'll send out some designers. You tell them what you just told me."

He shook my hand and left with his armed detachment of bodyguards.

The following day, many designers and surveyors arrived to discuss things with me; the following evening, President Jiménez called me, wanting to know how I made out. In a few days, a dozen heavy excavating machines and several explosion specialists showed up, and in a few months, my casual remark became a reality.

RETURN TO THE MAINLAND

At the beginning of August, my family came from the island on a fishing boat, hauling with us our accumulated household objects. Esbilia gave up her job as a dental assistant and enthusiastically assumed the responsibility of nursemaid, and the maid Maria stayed on with us as our housekeeper. We lived temporarily in an apartment in La Pastora, and after my second daughter was born on August 11, 1953, we rented a villa in the Corralito Mountains, near Los Teques. I named my daughter after my sister Vlasta, which translated from Czech is Patricia. I also hired a chauffeur. He was wonderful; he helped me with work around the house, was a great bartender, and even cooked Italian specialties for us, like his *pizza extraordinaire.*

We decorated our living room with hand-carved caoba (mahogany) furniture which a visiting Chinese princess had left behind. It was a fitting aesthetic addition, since it faced the large attractive veranda that overlooked the mountain range of Avila to one side and the Corralito Valley to the other.

The surrounding tropical forests were nothing short of paradise, and we also lived close to beautiful beaches, where I could dive and explore the underwater splendor. I had free time for woodworking and painting and made an attractive bar of caoba with lights and folding doors; it went well with the furniture that had belonged to the princess. Home life seemed steady and pleasant. My little family was thriving.

The construction of the building for the marines in Maiquetia progressed on schedule, and my exposure to the Venezuelan engineering community was well under way. Marcel supported me even more by introducing me to his friends and cousins, who retained me as a part-time consultant or designer. One assignment in particular gave me an opportunity to combine the mechanical engineering I learned in school with the civil engineering I learned in the field; I designed a machine to test soil for compression and shear for Marcel's cousin, who was contracted to study and test a stretch of the Pan-American Highway, including the construction of a steel bridge over the River Caroni. After the building of *Infanteria de Marina* was completed, I had already secured the job to test the soil for the Pan-American Highway and had reserved the job as a resident engineer of bridge construction over the River Caroni.

Before completion of the bridge in November 1953, when work was well under way, the Venezuelan Geodetic Department borrowed me from Marcel to establish benchmarks mapping the region south of the Orinoco River for the *Cartographia Nacional*. This work gave me an unforgettable hundred-day experience with one of the oldest human cultures in the world—the Yanomamo Indians. We hired natives to help us in the jungle, and my party of eight surveyors, helpers, and a cook covered the territory southwest from the Orinoco River and Cerro

Canapiare, already in Brazilian territory. We also worked the area at the borders of Brazil and the south end of the Parima mountain range where, we were told, the Orinoco River originated. The famous Pico de Neblina, discovered just a couple of years before we came there, was about two hundred miles southwest.

In March of 1955, Marcel assigned to me the inspection job of the "Vacation City of Los Caracas." I rented a nice villa in Naiguatá, which was just five kilometers from the job site, and about thirty kilometers from the Maiquetia Airport, and purchased a new car, a small, manual convertible English-made Singer.

President Jiménez came to see my project several times. He ordered the construction of several projects for the people, like Los Caracas, but those projects were intended for the ordinary employees of the government and also the city employees. When he visited, he brought gifts; once he brought eighteen-carat gold jewelry pieces with the Venezuelan coat of arms.

CHAOS—AGAIN

The last time President Jiménez came to see me was in January of 1956, and he told me I should follow the news closely. He said there was sure to be trouble and promised he would be in touch with me again.

As the President predicted, the political landscape in Venezuela began to crumble. I was very concerned, because I did not want to go through another revolution; having a family made me feel quite different about wars.

In Brazil, the city of Brasilia had started construction, so I contacted the embassy to find out more about it. Because there was nothing for us at the United States foreign office yet, I obtained documentation from the Brazilian consul, just in case. Their offer was favorable, and because we were both professionals, jobs were promised to be waiting for us.

I was in Marcel's office in Caracas during the last week of August 1956; he had gone to Cuba to offer our services to design and construct a large steel gate for a dam, and he asked me to cover for him during office hours. Suddenly, at around 11:00 a.m., he called me, frantic. "Take all of your money out of the bank and run! Don't lose any time! Run!"

I hung up immediately and ran across Chacaito Plaza, but I arrived too late; they were just locking the door of the bank.

The whole country was entering into turmoil, financial and otherwise, and a lot of money was lost that day. My loss was only about seventeen thousand dollars, but Marcel's was at least a million. I called him back only to learn that more trouble was coming. As I was packing up a few things in the office, the President's secretary called; then the President himself came on the phone to tell me to flee the country, for it was heading toward a revolution. I never heard from him again.

Later, in the papers, I read that he had left for the United States and the American government did not give him asylum. He was returned to Venezuela, tried, and convicted on charges of being a dictator, mishandling funds, and corruption.

According to that logic, all the previous presidents should have been imprisoned for life. The Venezuelan economy flourished under Marcos Peres Jiménez' presidency; in 1956 the bolivar was one of the most stable currencies on the international exchange, with one dollar equaling three bolivars. (By 2002 the bolivar had sunk to an unprecedented low and the national economy entered into bankruptcy). None of the accusations against President Jiménez were proven, so he was released; he retired in exile in Spain. I felt for him, for I knew he had meant well for the country; today one can hear much about his presidency, how good it was, and how the country has never been the same.

At the time, I was more concerned with my family's and my own welfare. For the first time since 1948, I felt the old, familiar fear of people rising up and fighting. Another revolution! People would never stop.

I made my way to the Brazilian Embassy. On Avenida Andres Bello, in the most urban quarter of San Bernadino, were several embassies. The last of the avenue was the Brazilian; the first was the American. I had gone there frequently to ask if our emigration papers had come through. The receptionist in the front office already knew me, and when I stopped and waved to her as I passed by, she waved back, holding an envelope in her hand. I parked, and when I walked through the door of the embassy she handed me our United States visas. It was unbelievable! Some might have thought it coincidence or fate, but I believed it was because of Valentina's action, registering on time. We could enter the United States any time we wished. I just needed to report to the Venezuelan Immigration Department to get a seal of exit, make a reservation with Pan American Airlines, and pay for the trip. We would fly to New Orleans, and from there Delta Airlines was to take us to Detroit.

I rushed home. I did not have enough money for the flight and no one to ask for help. Still, we began to pack. I disassembled the Chinese furniture, made packages, and hoped Pan Am would take it as cargo. The whole time I thought about our lack of funds. We were short at least six hundred dollars. I had no idea of what to do.

Even Esbilia tried to help. She went through the pueblo and advertised that we were selling our furniture, but nobody was interested in our stuff. Finally, one man came by and wanted to purchase the caoba bar. He paid me 2,500 *bolivars*, which worked out to be just what we needed.

The last night in Naiguatá we had a long conversation with Esbilia and Maria. We wanted to take Esbilia with us. Unfortunately, she couldn't leave her parents, and it was also impossible due to immigration laws. We would miss her greatly, for she was a shining example of purity and goodness in a Caribbean paradise.

On September 13, 1956, in the early morning, our friends took us to the airport. After five-and-a-half years, I left Venezuela with mixed feelings. The dismal past seemed to appear before me: escape from my homeland, refugee status in Germany, being a foreigner in Venezuela. And now, a potentially chaotic, uncertain future. I hoped for some fair play from destiny and that somehow I would find the normalcy I so ardently sought—and tasted for only a short while in Venezuela. Yet I knew there were no guarantees; all of my previous experiences had taught me that. Still, I thought to myself, as a small spark of excitement entered my heart, maybe now.

Later that day we were received in New Orleans as residents. With pride, I said a memorized phrase to the New Orleans customs official: "I will be a good American." I would never forget his inquisitive look, because he couldn't comprehend my pronunciation.

It took me eight years to reach the United States of America, but I never doubted I would make it. At last we reached the land I had hoped for since 1948.

eight

CITIZENS OF THE NEW WORLD

I grew up in "diversity"
And always liked to meet different people.
When I crossed borders.
I was also "the other"
And count myself among the different ones.

WE WERE FORTUNATE immigrants: Valentina's mother and her brother Gene were waiting for us at the Willow Run Airport in Michigan. In that moment, all of my patriotic loyalty transferred to the United States, and I became an American. I left my Czechoslovakian heritage in the old country where it belonged; I would always honor my parents and their heritage, as well as the country of my birth, but the changes I was making upon entering the United States were for keeps—forever.

Mrs. Vlasov and Gene lived in Detroit in a rented bungalow and were anxious to have us stay with them. For me, though, it was different; I keenly felt the need to have my family secure and in its own nest. However, I was just as bad off as when we had arrived in Caracas; again, I felt useless, for I didn't speak English. I didn't have a dime to

my name, and the streets of Detroit resembled those of Caracas—just as
strange, just as forbidding—when I looked for a job there.

In the beginning, right after our arrival, the benevolence of Mother
Vlasov was crucial to our survival. She did it solely for her daughter's
sake at first, but in the long run it also helped me and our children. Her
generosity and assistance made her worthy of my greatest esteem, and
I looked forward to having a chance to repay her many favors. From
what we were told by the authorities in Bavaria, my own parents were
dead, so I greatly needed someone for whom to care.

At first, Mrs. Vlasov did not like me much because I was not a
Russian and I was not an Orthodox believer; in fact, some people from
the camp in Bavaria where she stayed before immigrating to the United
States told her that her daughter had married a Jew. It should not have
mattered, but such were her thoughts. I had lost so much weight at
Lechfeld that I looked like an inmate from a death camp, and I'd never
completely recovered my former physique; it wasn't difficult for Mrs.
Vlasov to believe the rumors. The small talk did not bother me, since I
did not share her concerns or care of what others thought; in fact, I was
honored to be thought of as such a survivor.

Of course, it was Valentina again who came up with a viable lead
to help with our survival. She found an ad in *The Detroit News* in
which Congress Steel Products Company in Melvindale asked for a
"structural engineer for the design and detailing of structural steel."
We traced out a route to the company on the map, and early the next
day I set out to Melvindale on foot to find the company. Jobs, especially those for a newcomer, were hard to find; at that point, I would
have welcomed any way to support my wife and two young daughters,
who were just five and four years old. Although I was fluent in six
languages, I would have given all of them up for a minute knowledge

of English. I was gravely concerned about our future; it seemed somewhat doubtful until the end of October 1956, when things began to transform.

Melvindale was only eight miles from our Campbell Street residence, but walking through unknown territory was quite an undertaking. With a sandwich in one pocket and the newspaper ad with the address in the other, I left on this grand journey to change my destiny, or at least get enough change to feed us.

My inaccurate map and lack of English when I asked an occasional pedestrian for directions led me the long way around to the Congress Steel Products factory. I quickly lost my bearings in the maze of downriver streets, which all converged at the river without identification and spread to the northern adjacent communities, with changed numbers and street names. Finally, shortly before noon, I entered a field office adjoining a shop, from where loud hammering and the welding arcs suggested the manufacture of structural steel.

An accountant looked up from a pile of books when I entered and expected me to say what I wanted. My answer was almost as silent as his inquisitive look, but I showed him the small, carefully guarded ad and awkwardly pronounced the only word I knew, "Structural." My clumsy approach did not encourage him to make conversation; he simply pointed to a door where, I assumed, I would face a person who was looking for someone "structural."

My throat tightened and my mouth, dry by then, pronounced again the magic word when I met the chief engineer, Larry Snyder, a pleasant individual of about forty. I was encouraged by his friendly demeanor, and I managed to smile. That, of course, was not enough; I needed to explain my presence, so I pointed to the small ad again and managed an extremely simplistic almost-sentence, "I structural."

201

Larry's own smile froze. "Oh, shit," he said. "Another dumb Polack."

Luckily, I didn't understand what he said, though I felt that he was searching for an appropriate response to make me say more.

"Hmm . . . you structural?" he asked, then added a few more well-spoken comments; he was obviously an intelligent and articulate fellow. Much later, when I could appreciate good English, I admired his speech and turns of phrase. At the time, I was encouraged by his talk and could only assume he was discussing questions of employment.

He stood up and led me to a large cabinet full of drawings. I knew he needed to know about my knowledge of structural design. Scanning the drawer, I found familiar drawings of trusses and structural steel details. Upon seeing them I felt things were about to go well for me, and I hoped to get the job. Enthusiastically, I shouted, "I structural! I work!"

Larry, however, was less enthusiastic; I sensed he was worried about my English-speaking capabilities. But after more one-sided conversation, somehow I understood I had a job paying $2.75 per hour. Larry told me when I would start; he stepped over to a wall calendar, pointed, poked me in the chest with his finger and said, more than once, "You—work!"

The following Monday, I was there before the factory doors opened, and parked my borrowed Oldsmobile facing the Congress Steel Products complex, so I could take in the size and quality of the buildings. Soon, thoughts about my present situation took over, and I began to sort out the advantages and disadvantages; I now had a job, and figured that if I did it well, I would make friends.

When I met with Larry once more that first day and he showed me around a bit, I found that my confidence in the future was reaffirmed. Over the weekend I learned some English to impress Larry, but I was still a long way from a secure job, and a long way from knowing all of the tricks of the profession. I realized I would be facing some problems using the country's system of measurements; for me the metric system was a thing of the past. My engineering ability and my judgment of energy and force in design procedures, which I developed during my earlier training, became useless for a while. My skill in the sizing and proportioning of structural components lacked accuracy because I did not have a truly clear sense of foot-pounds. I felt quite insecure; to protect myself, I calculated all structures in both standard measure and metric measure to cross-check. Because of that I had to work harder, and calculations took me longer to complete. There were no electronic calculators.

I did make friends in the shop. The workers were good-natured and the few jokes to tease me were well meant. I learned much from them; although Larry gave me a structural manual with all the necessary guidelines, the practical observations and advice in the shop were priceless. The shop workers, many minorities or immigrants like me, and the well-qualified field erection teams, were my best teachers for English, though I later had to revise what they taught a little, using less profane expressions.

Things were also progressing on the home front. My brother-in-law had advised me on how to purchase a car so I could commute to work and help Valentina and Mrs. Vlasov with transportation. The job, which paid about $150 per week, combined with some moonlighting, elevated my credit rating. Soon we were able to purchase a new house in Allen Park, close to my office.

We bought from Sears the necessities to furnish the house, like the kitchen appliances, and dining room and bedroom furniture. Mrs. Vlasov helped with some linens, but we had to buy clothing. We were not ready for winter at all, since we had moved from the tropics. Sears gave us credit at once, because we had been their customers in Caracas.

I had to buy a drafting table for my moonlighting jobs, and Larry let me have the supplies I needed from the office. I worked ten-hour shifts at Congress Steel and at home in the basement for another four hours a day. The jobs I did at home were much more profitable than working for Larry; however, working for Congress Steel gave me more security and the insurance coverage we needed. I was pleased to discover, when I calculated our budget after Christmas of 1956, that we could begin to save for a rainy day.

In September of 1957, I matriculated in Wayne State University to study English for the foreign-born. The cost of the classes was negligible, but the time required to come and go to school became a serious burden, limiting my working hours and causing our income to decline. I had to work more at night, and my stress level increased, affecting my health. Still, in the English class I made remarkable progress, and I was able to take a class on highway engineering to get familiar with the Michigan highway construction practices. Being exposed to proper engineering language, I improved my ability to communicate with other profession- als. The classes helped my written expression, which came in handy later when I took the Professional Engineers' exam for state registration.

The year of 1958 was tough, and I doubled my efforts to earn more. Larry helped me get private jobs, and I worked evenings and weekends; he even searched for a better position for me elsewhere. He often said that I should be able to better myself and urged me to take the state exam to be registered in Michigan, stressing how important it was to have a license. (Finally, in 1971 I received the all-important state profes- sional engineer certification).

Our family of four increased to five on June 29, 1958, when my son Gene was born. Ironically, the family now had one American citizen and four foreigners: the two girls, who were Venezuelans; Valentina, who was Russian/Latvian; and I, a Czechoslovakian. Our own family epitomized the American melting pot.

On November 20, 1962, the rest of us became official United States citizens.

Another of my dreams had come true.

nine

THE POWER OF "IF"

I was educated as an engineer
To survive to make a living,
But it was always the love of my family
That has gotten got me through
To make a happy life.

I FELT LUCKY TO be in the United States of America. Whenever difficulties arose, I told myself to consider what was going on in the rest of the world—American Intelligence Service officials had told me in 1951 that my family in Czechoslovakia was dead, that I could not even write to anyone there. I knew in my heart that I should be happy; I had formed my own family, and done exactly what I was supposed to do, what my uncle had told me, "When it gets out of control here, leave this country, change your name, change your nationality, find a good wife, make your own family, and forget."

Why would anybody want to renounce a Motherland? Even though my life in Czechoslovakia was far from perfect, it once held the promise for me of great resources for learning. Once, any inquisitive mind wanting to satisfy the hunger for knowledge had remarkable opportunities to grow. But when the world was in flames, I gathered and preserved all I could; I never would have abandoned my country, save in a desperate act of self-preservation when the odds against me were overwhelming.

I did not have to change my last name when I became an American; I also would not forget.

Whenever I felt challenged, I also recalled what my father said. "Be honest and always tell the truth! Truth will overcome!"

I strictly lived by his words. And even now, safe and building a new life in the United States, I relied on Kipling's poem, "If," as much for its inspiring words as for the memory of my father teaching it to me and the faith he expressed in my ability to live up to its message.

> *. . . If you can trust yourself when all men doubt you*
> *But make allowance for their doubting, too,*
> *If you can wait and not be tired by waiting . . .*
>
> *Yours is the Earth and everything that's in it,*
> *And—which is more—you'll be a Man, my son!*

When I had been locked up and tortured in the Czech prison, and infested with vermin in Camp Lechfeld in Bavaria, these verses held me up and helped me to dare to hope; they still had the same effect in the New World.

WORK AND PLAY; REUNITING AND PASSING ON

When Valentina and I purchased our house on Vine Street in December of 1956, we made a significant decision about who would support the family and who would keep the home and primarily bring up the children. Of course, income was critical, but more important was the quality of the children's upbringing—it was our highest priority. Valentina gave up her career as a doctor, and our decision was the right one. We would produce four exemplary citizens, and eventually our decision brought us much of the success we enjoyed later.

Those years, between 1956 and 1971, brought very dramatic changes as Valentina and I began to fit into the free society. It was not always easy. We soon noticed that the interpretation of "freedom" by Americans was different from how we understood it, and we were bombarded with verbiage that had never before entered our vocabulary. We had a lot to learn.

Were we misfits of the war we had experienced? Perhaps, but we knew well that we would not have made it elsewhere. Hadn't we tried in Venezuela, and once again been stymied by a revolution? It seemed God finally brought us to a place where we could start all over.

Without my own parents, Valentina's mother helped to fill that giant void. Valentina's father passed away after just a couple of months in Detroit, succumbing to cancer. He had been a builder, skillful in all trades associated with construction; he was also very well educated, and spoke several languages. Valentina missed him tremendously, and therefore her mother's presence was even more precious.

My mother-in-law made an amazing impact on my life. After she got over her initial negative impression of me—and a bit of her prejudice, perhaps—my mother-in-law devoted her culinary expertise to helping me gain weight. Slowly but surely, she started to like and then to love me. I was skillful and efficient around the house; she had high regard for that, and used to say, "Charles has golden hands."

In addition to all the financial assistance she had given us while we were in Venezuela and again when we came to the United States, Valentina's mother helped us in many ways in our Allen Park home; in my opinion, she was the one with golden hands. She was an expert seamstress and did wonders, creating new attire for us all with an inexpensive sewing machine. We truly needed it, since much of the clothing we had brought from Venezuela was inappropriate for our chillier northern environment. Mrs. Vlasov was a capable manager of everything to do with a home; in this, she reminded me in many ways of my own mother.

Our memories of our loved ones behind the Iron Curtain never faded. Valentina began to correspond with her aunt, who lived in Rezekne, Latvia, and that revived our curiosity about the situation in Czechoslovakia. Valentina had never quite accepted that my family had perished. And I, too—I always secretly hoped against hope that somehow they managed to survive. One day in 1957, Valentina made a suggestion. "Why don't we send a card through my aunt, to your parents' last address?" Such subterfuge was the only way to get word in or out of Czechoslovakia.

In about three weeks, we had staggering news. In a carefully worded letter, my father indicated that both he and my mother had survived, that my sister Vlasta was also living, but remained in prison. Uncle Joe was dead; after a long incarceration, on November 12, 1952, the great resistance leader had been executed by hanging in the Pankrác prison in Prague.

It was incredible. It would have been impossible to describe my whirl of emotions: joy and wonder jumbled up with frustration, grief, and sorrow. The loss of Uncle Joe was especially bitter.

Over a number of years, we continued to correspond in the same cautious manner, and were able to learn of Vlasta's parole on October 29, 1959, after ten years and two months of imprisonment. Knowing the Czech government would never allow both my parents to leave the country at the same time—an invitation for defection—I asked my father to find out whether my mother could come to visit us, hoping, of course, he would also be able to do so soon thereafter. In 1965, my father finally arranged for her visit, provided the government could hold him as a hostage. We had to send return flight tickets and certify that we would be fully responsible for her.

Mother arrived on Halloween night, 1965. This was the most exciting event for us since we had arrived in the New World. All of us were so happy to see her; I was the happiest of all.

The last time I saw her was in 1948, in the marketplace of Valašské Meziříčí, when I was returning to Slovakia after the failed attempt to make some contacts for Pavel Kominek. So, once she had a day to relax after her long journey from Prague, we had much to talk about.

First was the mutual surprise at discovering we'd survived. My family only knew what Vlasta had told them when she read my alias in the papers, that I was among seventeen men executed for high treason in 1948. So, for almost ten years, they lived with the belief that I was dead. When they received my card, my father's excitement had been incredible, and he shouted with delight, "I knew it! The rascal! They never caught him and they never will; he knew how to pull the wool over their eyes!"

It was a day to remember for them; my mother wept as she spoke of it, and my father also cried, she said, as he read our letter.

Then my mother spoke of how, a couple of days after they received our letter, they were due to visit Vlasta, who was still in prison. They were only allowed to see her once every three months. They took our letter and the photograph we had sent with them.

When I asked my mother how she and Father had fared, she paused, and then spoke slowly. "As you know, we were already in trouble in 1948, when you disappeared. Our whole family was suspected when

Uncle Joe was first detained in Lvov and then deported in chains to Czechoslovakia. We knew nothing of you. The postcards you sent—or others sent for you—from Slovakia to Brno held the Communists off for only a short while; when the postcards stopped, the Brno police were looking for you everywhere. Our family seemed doomed; your father was fired, our property was confiscated, and we were placed in a cheap, one-room living space. They took everything from us, but luckily I had hidden some of our jewels, which I sold. For a while we had some money for food, though the Communists wanted us to starve; the pension they paid your father wasn't nearly enough to sustain us. They couldn't accuse him of anything; he was too smart, so they just tried to eliminate us somehow. They couldn't figure out how you disappeared; they knew you were out of the country, and even during Vlasta's trial it was mentioned that you were engaged in subversive activity. The prosecutor and judges used it against her."

I told my mother about how I returned from Slovakia through Valašské Meziříčí. I could barely speak of it, for it made me very emotional. She vaguely recalled seeing a young man in the market, but had no idea it had been me. My face had been so changed and, at the time, she had been mourning me as her dead son.

My mother continued to explain what happened during the intervening years. When, after July 27, 1948, the news about the execution of seventeen men condemned for high treason was printed in the newspaper, my parents were secluded in Valašské Meziříčí in a small, one-room living space assigned to them by the secretariat of the Communist Party. They were saddened and troubled; being close to retirement age, they had hoped for peace, but instead, this sudden shift in living standards had traumatized them. They began to feel the hostilities of the new regime; the insulting attitude toward them from those around them, equally enslaved by the current order, made my parents exiles in their own country. At first seen as liberators, the Communists insidiously increased their oppression of the Czech people. Eventually, the authorities confiscated my father's property and evicted my parents from their home on Mirova Boulevard. They were moved into a designated low-income neighborhood. Personal valuables, which they managed to conceal in time to avoid confiscation, were exchanged in secret for money to supplement their meager meals. The federal government at first gave my father a small pension, but it was the lowest in the federal pay scale, in spite of the fact that he had paid all his life premiums for the highest.

My mother, a proud Hungarian, and my father, a distinguished Moravian, held on to their self-respect and right to be free. They were crushed materially; but loyalty to their homeland, nurtured since childhood, kept their virtues and spirits high. They believed they had only suffered a temporary setback, and the future was bright despite declining odds.

Their steadfastness and strength were astounding, and this was why I loved my parents so. Most sons and daughters admire their parents; I worshipped mine. They were my genuine guides.

Our conversations went on and on. We stayed up late on many evenings, relating all that had befallen us. I could not get enough of speaking to her. At the end of February 1966, however, my mother returned to Czechoslovakia. The four months had flown.

We immediately started to plan to get my father to America. In the meantime, my son Alex was born in August.

Finally, on September 2, 1966, my father arrived. As my mother and I had done, so did my father and I relive the past. I had not thought my happiness at seeing my mother again could be equaled, but I was wrong.

Vlasta and I could only write to each other, and much of what we wrote had to be in code, since letters were censored.

While Valentina and I hoped for her arrival, we decided to reward ourselves for all of the work we had done since arriving in the United States ten years earlier. We took our first vacation, traveling first to Costa del Sol in Spain, and from there to Cadiz, Gibraltar, Marrakesh, Casablanca, and Tangier, where we sat in the Café Detroit and looked out over the harbor, as I remembered the trip I had made for Uncle Joe.

At last, in 1968 when Dubček came to power and Czechoslovakian restrictions were relaxed, Vlasta was permitted to visit us. It was another wonderful reunion.

After Vlasta returned to Czechoslovakia, however, our mother passed away on December 13, 1968. Her passing drove a deep hole into my heart, as if by a spear. I could not speak of it much then, and I still cannot do so.

My father came a second time to visit, this time in 1969—again, together, we saw history made as we watched the famous moon landing that July.

In November that year, Valentina, my son Gene, and I took a trip back to Europe, returning again two years later. We still could not enter Czechoslovakia, so we flew to Yugoslavia and met my sister and her husband Mirek there. Through an unusual coded correspondence, we could identify where in Yugoslavia we could meet without the Czech censors detecting why Vlasta requested a visa to travel with her husband. In 1971, Yugoslavia was a fine place to visit, and we toured many places we had visited with our father before the war.

In 1978, I arranged with Vlasta a meeting in the Yugoslavian city Rijeka, at a certain time and at the same hotel where our father used to play cards. These still were times when anything behind the Iron Curtain was untouchable; even so long after the resistance, I could not visit my family without possibly being arrested.

We moved from our Allen Park house to Southfield in 1970, and eventually we bought the property next door and rebuilt it for Mrs. Vlasov. It was then a difficult time for me, however, due to an automobile accident in which I sustained a closed head injury, creating terrible headaches. Still, I undertook the project for my mother-in-law, since she had been so kind to us all. Our time as neighbors was short, though—Mrs. Vlasov passed away on January 8, 1985. We would miss her ever after. Still, our lives went on, and we found ways to keep our sadness at bay.

ENGINEERING A CAREER

Through the years I had continued to experience growth in my chosen field. My career had started at Congress Steel, and with Larry Snyder's help, in 1960, I had gotten the job to construct Cobo Hall with the O.W. Burke Company. Undoubtedly, this was the springboard into my civil engineering career in the United States, and a few years later, when I became a registered professional engineer in Michigan, I had a list of significant projects in the state for which I was responsible.

After the Cobo Convention Hall in Detroit was finished in 1961, I was transferred from O.W. Burke Company to Darin and Armstrong as a coordinator and superintendent to construct the General Motors Ternsted project.

Following Ternsted, my projects continued to grow ever larger and more complex: Providence Hospital, Universal City Shopping Center, the Buick Administration Building in Flint, a General Motors marble palace that was finished in 1967.

After managing Minoru Yamasaki's Chrysler Styling Center project in Highland Park, I received a significant recognition in June of 1971 from the American Concrete Institute in San Francisco. Then came Washtenaw Community College in Ypsilanti, followed by Tower 14 in Southfield for Dayton Hudson. This was one of the first projects of its kind: a pre-cast masonry design erecting a floor every three weeks. Once the foundation was finished, the fifteen-story building was up in less than eleven months and the job was completed at the end of 1973.

Three major satellites for Henry Ford Hospital came next, then the Silverdome in Pontiac, the Oxford High School, and consulting for the Cranbrook Institute of Arts.

It seemed I had amassed an honorable list of engineering accomplishments. In November of that same year, I received the Distinguished Service Award from the Michigan Society of Professional Engineers; this recognition made me feel good about my profession.

Just before 1979, I was assigned to the City of Detroit as multiple projects administrator and consultant. Detroit's mayor, Coleman A. Young, had received from the federal government $42 million to renovate parts of the city. My employer, Barton Malow, was awarded the administration of eight separate projects throughout Detroit, with me as the construction administrator; the works began in the spring of 1979.

The projects were well under way when my head injury occurred, so I was kept busy enough to distract me from its painful aftermath. Problems with equal employment, unions, and keeping harmony among the city officials and architects mounted. By the time all of these projects were finished, sometime around the end of 1982, I became aware that I had, in fact, ceased to work as an engineer; I had instead become a peacemaker, holding different factions and races together, sometimes in seemingly hopeless circumstances.

The squabbling was exhausting. It felt to me that my life so far had been too frantic; even my childhood had been chaotic, and the war years were even more overwhelming. Even in the peaceful United States, I'd had to work hard to establish my family. Retirement began to look more and more attractive. I wanted a more relaxed activity, like painting or sculpting; my yearning for artistic endeavors continued to tug at me. And the head pains I experienced since my car accident had not diminished, and my doctor, my good friend Dr. Michael Grishkoff, did not know what would come of them; he referred me to a different specialist, Dr. Joel Saper, who had a head pain clinic in Ann Arbor. I tried to be an attentive and responsible patient, but found no improvement.

Aging was not proving to be a gentle process for me. Then again, is it for anyone?

Before I could make any decision, I was selected as quality assurance manager for the $250 million Detroit People Mover project, complete with a full staff of engineers and technicians. Aches and pains aside, I was elated. There was no way I could refuse; the job would have all the trimmings an engineer would desire to execute a really important project in exactly the way he had been trained to do it. This would be my final job prior to retirement and the highest position I had ever attained; even the project directors reported to me. The project functioned around the word "quality" in everything, starting with the design and ending with minutiae like signs on the doors. My attitude and behavior had to reflect the maturity expected of a person holding such a position. My father was often on my mind then, and his words from the past resonated in my thoughts with increasing clarity, guiding my actions throughout the project.

When the project was completed, I finally retired, separating myself from construction altogether. I even departed slowly from professional associations, and kept only my professional registration with its corporation seal—just in case.

With the hope of finer things, I began the next chapter of my life.

ten

PERSONAL PEACE, PERSONAL TURMOIL

I managed the construction of many structures
In downtown Detroit
And I am still supervising them,
Just keeping my eye on things.
Since I've retired, they've been neglected.
Hopefully, that will change.

RETIREMENT

VALENTINA FOUND PLENTY of activities for us to engage in during our retirement, and it was all exactly what I had been waiting for.

That same year, 1985, Vlasta and her husband Mirek came to visit us in June, staying for four months and living next door in Mother Vlasov's house. We traveled a great deal by car to show them our adopted country, and it was also a wonderful trip for us, since we had the chance to learn more about America. We traveled about fourteen thousand miles, from Detroit to the northern United States up to Oregon, and we visited all the national monuments along the way. Then we traveled along the west coast through San Francisco and Los Angeles, to Las Vegas and Colorado, and then Saint Louis, where we visited our son Gene and his wife Judy. When we returned to Southfield, it was time for Vlasta and Mirek to return home.

Except for family, we somewhat reduced our contacts with acquaintances, limited social engagements, and reorganized our home, where Valentina carried out her fur business, which she did mostly for fun. Since her childhood in Latvia, when she was exposed to fur coats and other fur garments, she had liked them and always wanted to play with them. We hired capable seamstresses and a housekeeper to allow more freedom for us.

We traveled a great deal, and we also registered for the 1986 school year at the University of Michigan's Dearborn campus, where we matriculated that same year as regular students. We received scholarships from the university's Retired Persons Program, so we paid only $50.00 per semester and could take any class we wanted either for credit or as auditors. The Bachelor of Arts in General Studies program we both took for a degree. After we graduated in 1989, we continued, but Valentina took courses for audit only, while I continued with credit courses. I had the motivation, but I also wanted to compare my performance with the other students. In our first year, for me the most important course of study was English, to enhance the language I had picked up so far and improve my grammar so I could write.

Several years before retiring, my contact with Cranbrook reawakened my artistic yen—especially my fascination with the figures of the Orpheus fountain—and I started to sketch Valentina in her long gown to outline her full-scale figure. I imagined her to be carved of limestone. As I child I had carved wood, trying to copy my father's woodworks on a small scale, and even then, stymied by lack of resources, I had yet wished to do works in stone. In Southfield, where I had space of my own and the means to let my fantasy wander into Michelangelo's

Renaissance, I pretended to myself that I could be a stone carver. After much labor, it appeared that I could indeed do it; it took me about three hundred hours to carve the statue of Valentina from an Indiana limestone block, and in 1979, I unveiled it amid much community and news media hoopla.

After I retired, I devoted even more time to art. I took a painting class from Electra Stamelos, and she and her husband Bill became our good friends. At her encouragement, I applied to Eastern Michigan University, where I participated in the Master of Arts program so I could finally get some formal training in painting. I believed then—and have continued to believe—that sculpting in stone or modeling clay were closely related to drawing and painting. It further occurred to me that these forms of creativity were just as closely affiliated with writing; to paraphrase Charlotte Brontë, if one can paint it, one should be able to write it. I received my Master of Arts in painting in 1993.

After 1991, when the Soviet Union collapsed, we were allowed to enter countries behind the Iron Curtain. For the first time since 1948, we traveled through Czechoslovakia, Russia, Latvia, Hungary, Poland, and many other places that had been prohibited to us for forty-three years.

While in Latvia, I was greatly moved by our visit to the Salaspils death camp. It seemed as if all the events that had transpired there came to life before my eyes. Our driver stopped and parked on the shoulder, and we walked to the sixty-acre death camp site, which was surrounded by eerie trees. The forest cast shadows upon the walk, making it even more chilling.

We passed by the camp marker to the gigantic concrete beam spanning over the entry, on which was carved these words: THE EARTH MOANS BEYOND THIS GATE.

The massive beam sloped from right to left with this ominous warning. The land was cut by it; on one side was life, and on the other was death.

As I walked into the camp I felt the beating of my heart, now synchronized with the electric metronome installed underground by the artist to connect vision and emotion. The enormous beam was supported on the right by a concrete building faced with a carved granite calendar of the years 1943 to 1944. Behind it, in the field, stood the stone epitaph constructed in memory of more than one hundred thousand people. Our driver explained that the exposed aggregate paved road, the pebbled surface on which we walked, symbolized the thousands of souls killed in that concentration camp. I froze then, for I felt I was walking over a thousand corpses; then I stepped over to the concrete paved edge constructed for that purpose. My blood pressure rose; the beating of my heart resonated in my bones and I felt the dead watching me and telling me of the horrible past.

I indeed heard the earth moan and I saw the indictment; I saw it in the weakened light of the falling sun, the indictment that had the form of a light and dark body, indictment carved in stone. During the last minutes of the sunset, the huge illuminated sculptures towered over the dark woods, and I found myself frightened and intimidated by the gloom. My imagination lured me into the nightmare, and I drifted back to 1943.

Terror controlled all. The barracks, overfilled with dying men, crying women and screaming children, surrounded me. Toward the east, against the sky, I saw the silhouette of the gallows. I stood in the shadow of the central watchtower, six stories high. Skeletons crowded the way to and from the shooting fields. Barbed wire fence around the camp, barracks, and the commander's building at the gate completed the image of carefully organized murder. The Nazi killing machine came to life in calculated detail.

I felt both numb and deeply troubled. In my mind, all the prisoners around me suddenly perished, but their hearts continued to beat. My heartbeat joined in rhythm with theirs and I, too, died. The sun fell and the camp darkened. Just the penumbra remained under the branches, and the weak light reflecting through the mist lit our way out to the road. I was speechless all the way to Riga and pondered why humans fell to such monstrous levels.

This was our first journey behind the Iron Curtain, and everywhere we went we found perversions and scars from the past, remnants of the Nazis and the Soviets. Saddened by all this, when we returned home I kissed the ground in my Southfield backyard.

OF LOSS

When we visited Moscow in 1991, Valentina's cousin, Dr. Tamara Artem'eva, and her husband Dr. Alexander Kovaljov, the Dean of Philosophy at Moscow State University, received us with open arms and introduced us to other faculty members. We stayed with Tamara and her husband at their Moscow State University apartment, and traveled the historical districts of Moscow. We rode an overnight train to St. Petersburg; there we stayed for about ten days, overwhelmed by rich history and tradition. Tamara, our devoted escort, who was a psychologist and also knowledgeable in Russian history, arranged and explained everything; we couldn't have had a better guide.

At the end of July of 1993, Tamara came from Moscow to visit us for three months, and we delighted in touring her around the United States. I made sure she would also have a permit visa to enter Canada, so we could show her both parts of the North American continent. All of these trips turned out to be very pleasant and beneficial for us, helping to learn more about American and Canadian geography and history.

However, driving through the beautiful Yellowstone territory, I noticed Valentina's relative indifference to her surroundings, stunning though they were. She had begun to show some signs of apathy the year before, but I chalked it up to the aging process.

After Tamara left, Valentina had two accidents driving. The first was when she drove the car out of the garage and scraped the side of it on the doorjamb. In the second, more serious one, she collided with another car that came at her from her left side. She simply didn't see it. Her peripheral vision seemed to be compromised. In this instance, both cars were totally destroyed, but thankfully neither driver was injured.

On December 1, 1993, we invited our English language professor, Betsy, for lunch to celebrate Valentina's birthday the next day. We had steaks and shared wonderful conversation about the class Betsy was teaching. Betsy left just after 7:00 p.m., and we began to get ready for bed and watch some television.

Suddenly Valentina's behavior turned strange. I did not suspect anything until I heard water spilling over the sink and flooding the bathroom. She had become ill, and vomit plugged the drain, and she stood there oblivious to what was happening. I carried her to bed and measured her blood pressure. Her speech was rambling and irrational.

Hospital tests revealed that Valentina had a brain tumor identified as an astrocytoma; its precise condition could only be determined surgically. She came out of the surgery fully conscious, once the anesthesia dissipated; her consciousness was due to relief of pressure after a partial tumor removal. It was not a solid mass, so some of it was impossible to remove and the doctor thought it would be treatable with radiation and chemotherapy. The biopsy seemed to show that the tumor was an unde-veloped and young matter that would be receptive to cure; however, Valentina's symptoms suggested otherwise.

Valentina knew already that her condition was terminal; the only question was how long she would be with us. Dr. Whitehouse told us that radiation and other treatment would extend her life somewhat, though he simply wasn't sure how long.

I brought Valentina home on December 14, with instructions to bring her daily to a local hospital branch for radiation treatments. I changed our bedroom into a hospital room, where I could administer all of the prescribed measures.

That Christmas we had all the trimmings, except for Valentina's usual loving personality and care. She was under constant pressure from the nagging knowledge of her inevitable and impending death, and on March 9, 1994, at the Angela Hospice in Livonia, she died.

When one's spouse dies, one goes around like a beheaded chicken and searches the endless labyrinth of the "unknown " for what once was a steady and reliable life. Those three months of Valentina's decline were the most difficult and terrible times of my life; not even prison, tor-ture, and waiting for execution in the Bohemian fortress were as cruel. Her death left me emotionally and physically devastated.

Now retirement, once longed for, seemed as if it would be an end-less sweep of loneliness.

In retirement everyone observes different signals, and most of the time we approach them unaware that soon severe changes will take place in our lives. Retirement could mean isolation, stopping work with others, and going it alone. It is harder than we expect, and the loneliness and sadness set in as we begin to hear our own requiem. It reminds us of an end that some of us thought we had foreseen in different colors, perhaps blinded by a vision of fun, partying, and forgetting that the inevitable may be just around the corner. One learns new drug vocabularies, ills, hospitals, and names of doctors. The conversations always end in words about disease or what the doctor prescribed. In the meantime medical bills keep rising and bank accounts keep dropping. The bang of sudden old age brings about a new index of priorities.

Such pessimistic views were coming upon me in force, and it was important to recognize them in time, before they caused permanent damage to me in a weakened state. I saw that, as Shakespeare noted—though in more eloquent terms—old age was just as wobbly as childhood.

Conditions in my home became unbearable; the house seemed empty and hollow, devoid of life. In the spring I completed a second stone sculpture, entitled "The Student," a portrait of Valentina sitting on a stump with a book in her hand. That was the only satisfying activity I had. After that, my efforts in painting came to a halt, and so did my studies. I could not produce anything, and I made more mistakes during the rest of that year than in all the years of my life combined.

I lost almost all the assets I had saved since the 1960s and was unable to coordinate my living. My dear dog Silva died, and I was utterly alone. It seemed that life itself had become a liability. My instinct for self-preservation slowly faded, and my hopes of surviving diminished.

I knew I had to come out of the depression and somehow formulate a program to change my conduct. The survival techniques I learned during the war returned to me, adapted for this new oppression. But loneliness was another matter.

I had to get out and see people.

At Schoolcraft College I started to study the Chinese language, and at the University of Michigan's Dearborn campus I continued to attend various classes. I started to paint, and then, to shake the pervasive sadness, I began to travel again. I also registered in a dating organization, hoping to find a new partner. I felt instinctively that Valentina would have wanted me to go on and have a normal, whole life.

So I packed and moved to the twenty-third floor at the Riverfront Apartments in downtown Detroit, where I transformed a large living room into my studio. But I needed a companion who would support me through the sad times, encourage me to study, give me confidence to write, and inspire me to continue my arts—not a replacement for Valentina, because no one can truly be replaced, but a partner who would be with me in this stage of life. During all this chaos, my friends Electra and Bill Stamelos remained true to and supportive of me, and through them in June 1996, I was fortunate to find the very partner for whom I dared to wish.

Sandy Scherba respected my sadness and supported me in my endeavors. If she were willing, I became dedicated to the idea of making a relationship with her work.

Sandy lived in her Victorian home in Fenton, which became the testing ground for our relationship. She was the director of the prestigious Cromaine Library in Hartland; I was impressed by her career accomplishments and state and national recognitions. She had even been the president of the Michigan Library Association.

Her intelligence and tender attitude toward me were very attractive. I was conscious of her own circumstances, and did not want to harm her. She had been divorced and was almost fearful of beginning a new relationship. Yet, in spite of all my concerns, I threw caution to the wind, and so did she. My destiny took me for a spin. Sandy and I married on October 21, 1996.

Starting a new relationship meant so much for us both that Sandy gave up her job as a library director and we both sold our houses, choosing to live in my apartment. We were fortunate in our try for a second time around.

However, I mismanaged my finances and lost most of what I had by the 1997 tax year; I was a victim of unscrupulous money managers, like many seniors throughout the country. To improve our cash flow we purchased a condominium on Cass Avenue, reducing our monthly payments and gaining about four hundred square feet of living space. I did not care for the condo, because of its surroundings, inadequate space for my work, poor interior finishes, and constant hassle with the developer/contractor. It was cost convenient, though, and in Midtown Detroit near the university, concert hall, art museum and opera.

For the time, it would be home.

THE YEAR 2000 AND BEYOND

After Sandy and I married, even as we lived in the Riverfront Towers, we traveled intermittently while I continued my studies at the University of Michigan.

Considering that Sandy and I had both been married before, we got along well. I both liked and loved Sandy, and was grateful she stuck with me through difficult times. I was certain that not everyone would have done so. My children had some hesitation about our relationship, but when they saw how much it heightened my morale, they began to care for Sandy. She had a good influence on me, and her family accepted me.

In December 2000 I graduated with a Master of Arts in Liberal Studies from the University of Michigan-Dearborn. Dr. John Kotre, my professor and advisor, deserved my sincere gratitude for his dedication in coaching me through a challenging program and showing me how to handle publishing a manuscript. The thesis, *Isla de Margarita: An Intimate Portrait*, my own book, was published that year.

I had hoped to continue toward achieving a doctorate in history, but my physical and mental condition stopped me. I would have to be satisfied with my three master's degrees, in engineering, fine arts, and liberal studies.

On our travels I introduced Sandy to my sister Vlasta and Uncle Joe's wife Helena in Brno and the many sites of my youth experiences; Tamara and "Sasha" in Moscow; and Oczi and Maruja Wolf and Esbilia Mata in Venezuela. She was also able to meet my Slovakian friend Valentine Burda when we journeyed to Isla de Margarita and flew via his home in Toronto.

On September 11, 2001, the World Trade Center towers were destroyed by terrorists and thousands of people perished. I never thought to relive any horror compared to what I had seen during the wars through which I had already lived, but this surpassed them. No words do justice to the sorrow that befell the city, the country, and the world on that day.

It never occurred to me during my younger years that life could be as different as the life I was living now. As I pondered the mystery of human existence, the choices narrowed to a simple process of comparing to others, which always ended with unanswered questions and made the mystery deepen even more. Discussions about such things with Sandy became a sort of tradition during our breakfasts, as we aired problems at hand, news stories, or controversies around the world.

At breakfast on Christmas morning 2001, Sandy and I debated how quickly time went by. I referred to the old adage: The older one gets, the faster time goes by. I thought that all this was relative. Sandy wondered what I meant, because my assertion was not clear enough. I knew that the reference to relativity needed more details and explanation, and even that still verged on the mysterious, because my claims merged into time and energy subjects that were sometimes unclear.

The time and energy in the infinite space were the same as the time and energy right there in our kitchen, I explained; so, it was perhaps relative to a size where it occurs. Was it possible that the time and energy during younger existence were relative to the older? Perhaps similarly, the speed during either time is also relative and we feel the inexplicable changes in how we perceive our own path through living. The speed was also a factor in the equation of relativity, because it was a component of energy and time; time might go quickly as one strives for or experiences happiness, and it might slow under the influence of ennui or angst.

Slowly I made these thoughts understood, both to Sandy and myself.

On January 29, 2002, another painful event came upon our family. In that day's early hours, Sandy's father, Eugene Gardulski, died in his home. I had come that morning to take him to the doctor. I was traumatized by finding him; yet the honor of being with him at that time would stay forever in my memory, for when my own father died I could not be with him.

During moments like these one's own mortality comes to mind, reminding us of how human existence evolves. I had fine memories of my parents, unforgettable times with my father and mother, and in their absence I had been fortunate to find new loving folk like Mrs. Vlasov, and Mr. and Mrs. Gardulski. Daily, as I drove by their residence, memories of them flowed through my mind. The golden years were distorted from how I perceived life, as biological ghosts unexpectedly began to delve deeper and deeper into my psyche, and I could size up the magnitude of it all. I had opened a can of worms by trying to penetrate my own mysteries to get out of frequent depressions, panics, and anxieties.

During these troubling attacks the time seemed to crawl by, emerging from the past and triggered by any former event, sense of taste, smells, or feelings.

At first I attributed these disorders to my older age, but soon I discovered that many younger persons were also troubled by them and I needed to redefine my ideas. Unknown to my untrained psychology, I stumbled onto Dr. Freud's lessons, going to and from doctors who only superficially helped with my recently diagnosed mental problems. In the past, these disorders were simply treated as madness, and those who suffered them were locked up in institutions; perhaps that was where I belonged, contradicting that ever-present golden years tag.

I worked through tribulations by writing. The best writers, like Gabriel Garcia Marquez, showed me how in their memoirs they crafted details and described the feelings and perceptions of their lives. I thought I could clear up much for myself, if I could write a journal entry each day. I didn't know what influenced my conditions: the old age, disorder in hormones, restricted brain neurotransmitters, or simple psychological chaos. I had felt tremendous sadness and uncontrollable grief when Valentina died; during the first months my mental stability was surely damaged and my reactions to my surroundings were irrational. I mismanaged everything around me until I met Sandy. By then, some permanent scars may have set in, never to be removed.

Still, life went on again. I felt I was slowly coming out of darkness, thanks to Sandy, who was very helpful and caring to me and made transitions easier. Ever energetic and always forging onward, she began to organize for me a show of my paintings at the Woods Gallery in the Huntington Woods Public Library. For it I prepared thirty-five paintings, all of which embodied the border crossings theme of the exhibit, which would last from February 17 to March 29, 2003. During the last few days before we were to hang the paintings, Sandy mentioned to me many times that I should paint a scene from Náměšt' nad Oslavou. For a couple of days I tried to recall what I could paint, so it would take on a true form. My memory was slowly fading, and I was afraid the landscape might have some flaws in it. However, I decided to paint the Baroque bridge with the statues, with the castle in the background; that scene I remembered best. It was a pen drawing with watercolor, as I only had two days to complete it. On Saturday, February 15, 2003, we hung the paintings prior to the show's opening. Later that year Sandy helped arrange another exhibit at the Ellen Kayrod Gallery in Midtown Detroit.

I knew that the theme—the crossing of borders—was not merely the theme of the exhibit. It was the overarching theme of my life.

I thought that perhaps I had more borders to cross over.

EPILOGUE

I N 1991, WHEN Valentina and I drove through Hrachovo, we found that a new post-tensioned pre-cast concrete bridge had replaced my father's old wooden one, but I was able to retrieve a small piece of wood from the original pilings still lodged in the riverbank, and which, being submerged, had been preserved from rotting.

Now, this old man looks back at who he was as a child of seven, remembering how he felt then and applying those feelings to the present. He finds that not much has changed. The world is still in disorder. Feelings from the man's past rise up again; they are lodged deeply in his soul. With the eyes of a child and without bias, the old man sees the past more clearly and today's viewpoint begins to merge with it, coloring the present with energy on one side and sadness on the other, sadness for the passing times and the loss of youth.

Today we face unsolvable anxieties as our society hopes for deliverance and finds only new hopelessness. However, why are we concerned about deliverance in the "land of plenty"? I think something went wrong along the way; somehow we misgauged freedom, and the nation abuses it.

We are failing in the important issues, like education, and in our convictions about quality and discipline. We politicize our social needs to the point where millions are harmed and, worse, where our destiny as a nation is threatened. Other nations seem to show qualities we used to defend, while we waste our good fortune on unessential power struggles and self-indulgence. Our world is fortunate to have been given rich diversity of animal life, splendor of vegetation, opulent colors, and an endless spectrum of natural resources from our Creator; to what use are we putting them?

The illumination of knowledge has blessed us thus far. We just have to place it in a perspective to reach Goodness; this Goodness, written with a capital "G," occupied the minds of Socrates and Plato as they sorted out what existed in the wide world for us. We just have to reach for it, reach for the Light from the cave of ignorance. We must free ourselves from the shackles of darkness, allow the Light in, and encourage the Good across our gulf of differences. We must sail on, together, as we were created.

I think back on my historic and emotional arrival in my chosen country, the United States of America.

Before I reached the border that day, I made it clear to myself that this would be for keeps. For me, it meant changing loyalty from Czechoslovakia to the United States, having America as my new Motherland. If she needed me, I would die to defend her. I felt that way when I entered in 1956 and today, as escalating anxiety and conflict threaten her freedom, I still feel ready to defend her.

It was not easy to make a covenant of that magnitude, but I knew then that I would never reclaim the country of my birth. The tragic past I would set behind me forever, and would write about it only to benefit the young; perhaps they could learn from it and avoid another war.

I remember puzzling that New Orleans customs official with my garbled promise: "I will be a good American." I have lived almost half my life as a Czechoslovakian and half as an American; to each Motherland,

I gave my committed efforts and my heart. Remember Kipling? "If you can keep your head when all about you are losing theirs . . . "

A lifetime has passed, and those words still resonate with their original energy, having supported me during all the wars and all the challenges, and having carried me, undaunted, across so many remarkable borders.

END

"The love of one's country is a splendid thing
But why should love stop at the border?"

—PABLO CASALS

TIMELINE

THE STORY OF Charles Novacek's life is inextricably interwoven with the story of Czechoslovakia, which for much of the twentieth century found itself a pawn in the machinations of powers beyond its own borders. Included in the timeline below are those milestones in twentieth century Czech history that particularly affected Charles Novacek and his family.

Many nations, ethnic and religious groups (especially the Jews), resistance fighters, and other individuals suffered heavily because of Nazi aggression. The timeline is in no way meant to be construed as a comprehensive review of the war or the enormity of its effects. Rather, it reflects the experience of one man and his family, who fought for Czechoslovakia's freedom as patriots whose awareness of the widespread devastation was limited, as it was for many, by the communication technology of the time, and by the impositions of war itself.

1916   Tomáš Garrigue Masaryk, Milan Štefánik, and Edvard Beneš help
          form the Czechoslovak National Council in Paris.

1917   Czechoslovak Corps in Russia form from several rifle brigades,
          organized to fight on behalf of Allies against Austria-Hungary.
          Eventually this "Czechoslovak Legion" numbers almost 40,000
          men.

1918   Following the collapse of the Austro-Hungarian Empire at the end
          of World War I, the Republic of Czechoslovakia is formed under

the Treaty of Versailles. Tomáš G. Masaryk is named its first president. The new republic comprises Bohemia and Moravia (including the primarily German and heavily industrial Sudetenland), plus Slovakia and (in 1919) Carpathian Ruthenia. The mix of ethnicities include Czech, Slovak, Hungarian, German, Ukrainian, and Polish.

1920   Amid increasing tensions with the Bolsheviks, and after prolonged negotiations and setbacks, the remainder of the Czechoslovak Legion leaves Russia for home in Czechoslovakia. To get home, the Legion travels across Siberia by railroad, across the Pacific Ocean by ship to the U.S.A., by train across U.S.A., by ship to Europe, and then by train back to Czechoslovakia. Charles Novacek's father is a member of the Czechoslovak Legion.

1928   Charles Novacek is born in Ožd'any, in the district of Rimavská Sobota in southern Slovakia. His father is by this time a police officer and his mother is a Hungarian born in Slovakia.

1931   Novacek family moves to Svatý Ondřej nad Hronom in northern Slovakia.

1933   JANUARY 30: Adolf Hitler comes to power as chancellor of Germany.

1935   OCTOBER: Novacek family moves to Hrachovo in southern Slovakia.

1935   DECEMBER 18: Edvard Beneš becomes Czechoslovak president upon Tomáš G. Masaryk's resignation.

1937   SEPTEMBER 14: Founding father and first Czechoslovak president Tomáš G. Masaryk dies.

1938   MARCH 12: Austria is annexed to Germany in the political maneuver known as the Anschluss, one of the first major steps in Hitler's campaign to build an empire. The Anschluss positioned Germany for subsequent land seizures and invasions and for an eventual attack on Russia.

1938   SEPTEMBER 29: Using complaints by Sudeten Germans of Czech prejudice as the ostensible motivation, Germany first attempts seizure by diplomatic measures, then threatens to invade the Sudetenland, identifying the heavily fortified area of Bohemia and Moravia as probable obstacles to their plans for empire. The Munich Agreement is signed by Adolf Hitler, Neville Chamberlain, Benito Mussolini, and Edouard Daladier and forced upon Czechoslovakia. The British inform President Beneš they are unwilling to go to war in defense of Czechoslovakia. The Sudetenland is ceded to Nazi Germany to "prevent" war.

1938   OCTOBER 5: President Edvard Beneš flees to London and sets up a Czech government-in-exile.

1938   NOVEMBER 2: Vienna Arbitration is forced upon Czechoslovakia, ceding large (ethnically Hungarian) areas of Slovakia and Carpathian Ruthenia to Hungary. Remaining Slovaks begin expulsion of Czechs, Hungarians, Gypsies, and Jews. The Novaceks are expelled to Náměšt' nad Oslavou in Moravia, near the birthplace of Charles' father.

1938   NOVEMBER 30: Emil Hácha is appointed president of the Czechoslovak Republic, with the promise from Hitler of a "tolerable" treatment of Czechoslovakia. His cooperation with German occupation is later seen as the only way he believed he could help the Czech people.

1939   MARCH 14: Under pressure from Hitler, independent (German puppet state) Slovak nation is declared.

1939   MARCH 15: Hitler breaks his promise of peace. Nazi Germany invades and takes over all of the remaining Czech lands as the "Protectorate of Bohemia and Moravia." Czechoslovakia becomes an occupied country.

1939   AUGUST 23: Germany and Soviet Union sign Non-Aggression Pact (the Molotov-Rippentrop Pact). In addition to stipulations of neutrality in the face of third-party invasion, the treaty included language dividing northern and eastern Europe into German and Soviet spheres of influence.

1939   SEPTEMBER 1: Germany invades Poland.

1939   SEPTEMBER 3: Britain and France declare war on Germany. World War II begins.

1939   OCTOBER 28: Medical student Jan Opletal is wounded in anti-Nazi demonstration in Prague and later dies on November 11.

1939   NOVEMBER 17: Nine Czech students protesting at Jan Opletal's funeral are executed, 1,200 students are sent to concentration camps, and many Czech universities and colleges are closed.

1941   JUNE 22: Germany violates Non-Aggression Pact by invading the Soviet Union.

1941   SEPTEMBER 27: Reinhard Heydrich is appointed acting Protector of Bohemia and Moravia, tightening Nazi control.

1941   DECEMBER 11: United States enters World War II.

1942   JANUARY 20: Reinhard Heydrich holds the Wannsee Conference with Nazi leaders to coordinate the "Final Solution of the Jewish Question."

1942   MAY 27: Nazi Protectorate head Reinhard Heydrich is attacked by the Czech Resistance in Prague and dies from blood poisoning on June 4; the villages of Lidice and Ležáky, in East Bohemia are destroyed by the Nazis in retaliation for Heydrich's assassination.

1943   NOVEMBER 28: Roosevelt, Churchill, and Stalin meet at Teheran.

1943   DECEMBER 12: Edvard Beneš signs a friendship treaty with the Soviet Union creating closer economic and military relations.

1944   AUGUST 29: The Slovak National Uprising occurs, centered in the city of Banská Bystrica, against the Nazi regime installed in Bratislava.

1945	FEBRUARY 4-11: Roosevelt, Churchill, and Stalin meet at Yalta to discuss the direction of the war. Decisions made at Yalta lead to Soviet forces being first to enter Berlin and set the stage for the "Iron Curtain."
1945	Czechoslovakia is liberated from Nazi Germany with help from the United States and the Soviet Red Army.
1945	APRIL 30: Adolf Hitler commits suicide.
1945	MAY 8: Germany surrenders to the Allies.
1945	MAY 10: Russian troops "liberate" (occupy) Prague.
1946	Decrees of Nationalization are declared by Czech President Edvard Beneš, resulting in most people of German background being expelled to Germany.
1947	Czech resistance to Communists begins to form.
1948	FEBRUARY 25: Communists seize power in Czechoslovakia in a coup d'etat.
1948	MARCH 10: Jan Masaryk, Czech foreign minister, dies under mysterious circumstances; Edvard Beneš resigns; the Communists take over the government.
1948-1989	Communist rule of Czechoslovakia.
1948	JUNE 14: Ardent Communist Klement Gottwald becomes president following the resignation of Edvard Beneš. Gottwald institutes a series of purges to eliminate Czech nationalists and prominent Czech Communists who oppose Russian influence.
1948	NOVEMBER 13: Charles Novacek escapes Czechoslovakia by crossing the border into Germany.
1949	Josef Robotká and Vlasta Nováčková are arrested, tried, and convicted of espionage and crimes against the state. Both are

sentenced to death; Vlasta's sentence is commuted to eighteen years hard labor.

1952   NOVEMBER 12: Josef Robotká is executed.

1959   OCTOBER 29: Vlasta Nováčková is released from prison.

1989   NOVEMBER 9: Berlin Wall is torn down, as communism crumbles in Eastern Europe.

1989   DECEMBER 4: State borders are opened.

1989   DECEMBER 29: Vaclav Havel is elected President of Czechoslovakia, replacing Gustav Husák.

1990   Vlasta Nováčková Jakubova is "rehabilitated" and receives recognition for her service to Czechoslovakia.

1991   Josef Robotká is promoted posthumously to rank of Brigadier General In Memoriam.

1997   OCTOBER 28: Josef Robotká receives the highest Czechoslovakian honor, the Order of the White Lion.

2007   JULY 13: Charles Novacek dies in Detroit, Michigan.

BIOGRAPHIES

VLASTA JAKUBOVÁ, (1925–)

V LASTA JAKUBOVÁ, NEE Nováčková, was born to Antonin and
Maria Nováček in Ožď'any, Slovakia, on March 13, 1925. Her
brother Karel (Charles) was born in 1928. A sister Lenka (Ilonka) born
in 1924 died fourteen days after birth.

Vlasta was thirteen years old when the
Munich Agreement gave the Sudetenlands
of Czechoslovakia to Germany, resulting
in the almost immediate German occupation of Bohemia and Moravia. Only
months later, the Vienna Arbitration
forced Czechoslovakia to cede large (ethnically Hungarian) areas of Slovakia and
Carpathian Ruthenia to Hungary, after
which the Germans declared Slovakia an
independent nation and the remaining

*Vlasta Nováčková and bicycle for
her courier work.*

Slovaks expelled Czechs, Hungarians, Gypsies and Jews. The Nováček
family was sent from Slovakia to Náměšt 'nad Oslavou in Antonin's
native Moravia.

Josef Robotká, Vlasta's first cousin once removed, fondly referred
to as Uncle Josef, was a key figure in her early life. A founding leader
in the underground resistance to the Nazis, Robotká enlisted the help

of Maria and Antonin Nováček; eventually, their children Vlasta and Karel joined the effort as well. At age fourteen, working for her uncle's Rada Tří (R3) guerrilla organization, Vlasta became a courier on bicycle and on foot. Little more than a girl, Vlasta wasn't suspected of performing undercover activities and so she succeeded in carrying messages between agents, penetrating communication blocks, and accomplishing other tasks that had proven impossible for male agents.

Like her brother, Vlasta managed to attend school despite the disruptions of war and her political commitments, and she graduated from the business academy in Trebic in 1945. She then returned to Slovakia to stay with friends, and in April of 1946, she received the Czechoslovakia Medal of Merit, First Class.

Following the war, Vlasta rejoined the resistance when the Communists took over Czechoslovakia. Under her uncle's direction, she gathered and delivered military, industrial, and economic information to agents within the country as well as to resources outside the Czech borders. She was trained to work with ciphers, so she was able to draft her messages in code, using invisible ink; for direct communication, she was also trained to use signals and sign language. Vlasta feigned a relationship with a man in the Netherlands to get the letters delivered to the resistance working from there.

In July 1949, Uncle Josef was kidnapped, interrogated and imprisoned for his resistance activities. A month later on August 6, 1949, Vlasta was seized at a factory office in Brno, where she worked as a secretary. The communist police took her to her apartment where they searched for subversive materials, confiscating her typewriter, chemical matches, chalk, papers, travel card, air-mail envelopes, and her passport. They also seized, according to records, a "workbook of Karel Nováček No. 280511723." Hoping her boyfriend would see the message, she wrote,

"I've been arrested," on the bathroom mirror. Then the authorities took her to jail on Orli Street in Brno, where she was interrogated, tortured, and placed in solitary confinement.

The mirror message failed, and it was six weeks before anyone realized her situation; friends thought she was traveling out of town. Any efforts they may have made to free her are undocumented. Meanwhile, Vlasta was being interrogated by up to seven people at a time. Afterward, she only fleetingly mentioned beatings and being tied; however, her general reluctance to talk about this period might indicate she was understating her treatment.

In this prison, she shared a large cell with other women, who all worked at such menial tasks as peeling potatoes, making insoles, and gluing boxes together. During occasional visits outdoors, she communicated in sign language with men prisoners she had known through the resistance; she was shocked by the poor condition of many.

As though their treatments weren't sufficiently inhumane, from the cell windows the women could see the place of the gallows. There were still executions going on in Brno at that time, and when an execution was occuring the windows in their rooms were covered over with lime. Vlasta did note later that the worst feeling was when they heard the hammering as the gallows were being constructed.

Vlasta was tried as part of Josef Robotká's group. The trial by the military senate in Brno ran only two days, from May 26 to May 27, 1950. The proceedings were secret and relatives were allowed to be present only for the verdict.

It was the judgment of the state court of Brno that Vlasta Nováčková was guilty of conspiring with Josef Robotká to reveal to foreign forces certain military and political facts deemed state secrets by the government, and for this act, entered into a relationship with foreign agents.

Court records indicate that the "accused Vlasta Nováčková defended herself by only saying that the reason she did it was that her Uncle Josef Robotká made an impression on her, that she took quite a fancy to him in the fight during the Nazi occupation during World War II, and that she would do anything for him." She admitted no regrets, nearly (some witness reports said) causing her legal advocate to faint in the courtroom).

First sentenced to death, Vlasta's ultimate punishment was set at eighteen years of hard labor, "intensified with one hard bed for six months and...a financial penalty in the total of 20,000 crowns." All her property was confiscated. Of the entire company arrested together, the only one to receive an uncommuted death penalty was Josef Robotká.

Women under these conditions endured horrific treatment. Typical torture and humiliation included beating, hair-pulling, electric shock, intense electric lights, cigarette burns on sensitive body parts, enforced nakedness, even rape. Vlasta has declined to discuss such treatments.

Although she and Uncle Josef were confined for a while at the same prison (where they communicated by sign language), Vlasta was moved throughout her sentence from prison to prison all over the country, incarcerated by turns in Cejl, Znojmo, Ruzyně, and Pardubice and work camps at Minkovice and Chrastava. Her family and boyfriend were allowed limited access; after six years, Vlasta broke off the relationship with her boyfriend, feeling it was "going nowhere." Vlasta formed an association of women prisoners with whom she still associates today, via annual reunions, shared travel, and other activities.

In 1959, Vlasta's kindness to another prisoner brought an unexpected reward, her early release from prison. While brewing chamomile tea for a friend at the factory where she and other prisoners worked, she incurred burns which resulted in hospitalization. The injury allowed her to be released early to recuperate under her parents' care in Valašské Meziříčí. So, on October 29, 1959, after serving ten years and two months, Vlasta was at last free. She was thirty-four years old; in one way or another, she had spent twenty years of her life in loyal service to the values of the country of her birth.

Two years later, she secured a three-room flat in Brno for herself and her parents to share. She worked first as a lab tech in a dairy then found a job in an engineering plant where she ultimately became a crane driver. In 1964, Vlasta married Mirek Jakub, who had also been a political prisoner, and like her, sentenced to eighteen years of hard labor. They had no children; Mirek died in 2010.

In 1968, Czech president Svoboda granted Vlasta amnesty and pardon, and allowed her to visit her brother in the United States. In 1990—some forty-one years after her infamous arrest and incarceration—Vlasta Nováčková Jakubová was at last "rehabilitated": recognized by her nation as a partisan and fighter for freedom and democracy. With her rehabilitation came an avalanche of honors for all the years of her resistance and incarceration.

Sources:

Pinerová, Klára, Fieldworker, "The Interview with Vlasta Jakubová," recorded in Brno, Czech Republic, August 17, 2008, and July 7, 2009. The interview is archived in the Oral History Center (COH) in Prague and was also published on the websites http://www.politictivezni.cz and http://www.politicalprisoners.eu and in the book: Bouška, Tomas, Klára Pinerová, and Michal Louč. Českoslovenští političtí vězni: životní příběhy. Prague, 2009.

Šmelová, Ivana, "Osudy politických vezenkyn v letech 1948-1960 [online]/The Life of Female Political Prisoners Between 1948 and 1960." (Diplomová Práce Masarykova Univerzita, Filozofická Fakulta, 2007) 12-19, http://is.muni.cz/th/65117/ff_m/Diplomova_prace.pdf.

JOSEF ROBOTKÁ (1906–1952)

JOSEF ROBOTKÁ WAS born on February 25, 1906, in Tasov in the Třebič district of the Vysočina region of Moravia. He was the son of an innkeeper and had two siblings—a brother František and a sister Marie. In September 1925, after graduating from secondary school in Velké Meziříčí, he voluntarily signed up for the armed forces and began studying as an army academic at the Military Academy in Hranice. He was discharged from there two years later as an infantry lieutenant and was attached to the Third Border Battalion in Žamberk. In September 1927, he was sent as a trainee to a training school in Milovice. When he returned, he was assigned as a platoon commander to the Thirty-Ninth Infantry Regiment in Bratislava. In 1931, he completed a three-month course for aircraft observers and was subsequently assigned

Josef Robotká

to the Second Air Force in Olomouc. His sojourn with this unit was short-lived, however. At his own request, he was discharged from the air corps and he returned to his previous post. In 1932, he was promoted to the rank of First Lieutenant, then married Helena Schneibergová on May 5, 1933. After successfully finishing another course for infantry officers, he was sent to the Military University in 1935. He successfully completed his studies in April 1938 and was assigned to the command of the Sixth Army Corps in Košice. By that time, he already held the rank of Captain, which he had obtained a year previously.

Josef Robotká returned to his parents in Velká Biteš when the Czech lands were occupied by Germany, and Slovakia was declared as an independent state. After the disbandment of the army, he entered the civil service, where he began working as an administrative superintendent, initially with the district authority in Tišnov and later with the authority in Valašské Meziříčí. By that time, however, he had already become involved in resistance activity as part of the Brno branch of the National Defense underground military organization. Upon the arrival of Reinhard Heydrich as Reichsprotekor in the autumn of 1941, he left his post at his own request and began working at the municipal savings bank in Brno in 1942. After a few months, he also quit this job and "ostensibly" became a forestry worker. He went underground in the spring of 1944. In the summer of 1942, he established contact with General Staff Captain Karel Steiner-Veselý, General Vojtěch Luža, and Professor Josef Grňa. Together with them he gradually built up a new organization known as the "Council of Three" ("Rada Tří"- R3) from the remnants of the original resistance movements. He was originally a political leader for this group before becoming the military representative for Moravia after the death of General Luža. He was awarded many honors for his activities during the war, including a Czechoslovak Military Cross 1939, a Czechoslovak Medal for Bravery in the Face of the Enemy, a Czechoslovak Medal of Merit of the First Degree, a Soviet Medal for Victory Over Germany, and a Czechoslovak Partisan Badge.

After the war, Josef Robotká joined the army once more in May 1945. This time he was stationed in Military Area 3 (VO-3) in Brno. In the interim, he was also retroactively promoted to the rank of Lieutenant Colonel of the General Staff. Despite this, he was unhappy with the new situation and found it particularly difficult to tolerate efforts by Communists to play down and raise doubts on the role of R3 in the anti-Nazi resistance, which manifested itself in the trial of Viktor Ryšánek, an informer for the Gestapo in Brno. Moreover, Robotká also criticized the manner in which important posts were filled. This was perhaps the reason why his application to join the Czechoslovak Communist Party was rejected, which should have been a warning signal. In March 1947, he was sent to the Voroshilov Academy in Moscow, but he did not complete his studies and was sent back to Prague on January 7, 1948, as an undesirable person by the Soviet authorities, together with Lieutenant Colonel Frantisek Skokan. He was subsequently transferred to the VO-2 Military Area in Tábor before being reassigned after the communist seizure of power in 1948 to the Twenty-Fourth Infantry Regiment in Znojmo, where he worked briefly as a battalion commander. Because of health problems, he was sent to a military hospital in Brno in April 1948. After that, he spent a month at the spa in Trenčianské Teplice, and was given three months sick leave in August. During this period, he was under complete surveillance by the defense intelligence authorities, and it was only a question of time before he was dismissed from the army as an undesirable element. This eventually happened on October 1, 1948, when he was placed on enforced leave. He was finally discharged in June 1949.

The final acts of Josef Robotká's life were typified by his return to resistance activity, although this time it was naturally directed against "red" totalitarianism. Through the intermediary Rudolf Boleslav, he managed to establish contact with the center of resistance, which had already been set up in Frankfurt in conjunction with the American CIC Intelligence Service by Robotká's acquaintance, the former General Staff Lieutenant Colonel Alois Šeda. He subsequently sent reports to this center containing political, economic, and military information, using both couriers and airmail dispatched via Holland. The letters appeared innocuous at first glance. But text was always written between the lines in "invisible" ink. In order to ensure sufficient supply of important intelligence material, Robotká set about building up a reporting network (although this was definitely not similar in nature to the type of system subsequently established by the Secret Police). This network was primarily composed of people he knew from the time of the German occupation. The opposing camp did not remain inactive, however. On April 1, 1949, the military authorities managed to arrest Milan Šeda (a nephew of Alois Šeda), who had returned to Czechoslovakia as a cross-border agent. His testimony was the basis for the gradual arrest of leading figures in the resistance movement. Josef Robotká's turn came on July 25, 1949.

After a long investigation lasting nine months, which was conducted using the usual Secret Police methods, Josef Robotká and eleven other people were brought before a panel of judges at the State Court in Brno (with Antonin Piak as the presiding judge and Antonin Mykiska as the prosecutor). After an in-camera trial process, which bore all the hallmarks of a political trial (among other things, it found that R3 was a Gestapo organization), Robotká was sentenced to death as one of this group for the crimes of treason and espionage. He was also stripped of his civil rights and forfeited all his property. When the Supreme Court dismissed an appeal and clemency was denied, the end was inevitable. Despite the fact that the execution was put off for a long time (primarily because of the Secret Police's incessant interest in him), the worst eventually happened on November 12, 1952, when General Staff First Lieutenant Josef Robotká was put to death in the early hours of the morning.

Josef Robotká was posthumously rehabilitated after the fall of the communist regime, and in 1991 was promoted to the rank of Brigadier General in memoriam. Furthermore, on October 28, 1997, the president of the Czech Republic awarded Robotká the Order of the White Lion,

Third Class, the highest order of the Czech Republic. His wife Helena accepted the award on Josef's behalf.

Sources:

Originally published in a slightly different form in "Documenting the People Executed on Political Grounds in the Years, 1948-1989, Josef Robotká (1906-1952)," Institute for the Study of Totalitarian Regimes, 2012. http://www.ustrcr.cz/en/josef-robotka-en by Mgr. Daniel Herman. Reprinted by permission of the author and the publisher.

HELENA ROBOTKOVÁ (1910–2005)

H ELENA ROBOTKOVÁ, NEE Schneibergová, was born in Velká Bíteš, Czechoslovakia, on December 1, 1910. Her father František Schneiberg was a military physician. She married Josef Robotká in Bratislava on May 5, 1933, and shared with him the uneasy fate of soldier, resistance fighter, and alleged traitor through her work in the Czech Resistance during World War II and the Cold War. Her primary involvement was in the Obrana Národa (Defense of the Nation), Rada Tří, and assisting with the discovery in 1944 of Gestapo agent/informer Viktor Ryšánek.

On May 9, 1945, during the day of liberation of Velká Biteš from the six-month German occupation, Soviet tanks were rolling into the town from Brno. Helena and Josef

Josef and Helena Robotká, 1933.

were joyfully waving the Czechoslovakian national flag when their house was suddenly bombed by the Russians. Helena was pulled from the rubble seriously wounded. A year later, when finally recovered, she contracted typhoid fever. Helena was forced to reduce her involvement in resistance activities.

One evening in July 1949, Robotková's husband left home in Velká Bíteš for an appointment, telling his wife he would return in half an hour. Instead, he was arrested and imprisoned by the Communists. The couple found a way to send secret messages to each other that they then destroyed immediately after reading. Robotková was finally able to visit her husband when his trial was held in May 1950. They were under strict supervision and Robotká could not tell his wife he had been sentenced to death in a secret prison tribunal.

Helena was allowed a controlled visit with her husband shortly before his execution at Pankrác Prison in Prague on November 12, 1952. Josef's ashes were buried in an undisclosed location in Prague Ďáblice. Ironically, Helena was asked by the State to pay his funeral expenses.

Helena Robotková died on January 24, 2005, in Brno, Czech Republic, nearly fifty-three years after her husband was convicted of treason and hanged.

Sources:

Kopečný, Petr. "Helena Robotková: 1.10.1910 – 24.1.2005." Město Velká Biteš, http://www.vbites.cz. 2005.

Luza, Radomir with Christina Vella. *The Hitler Kiss: A Memoir of the Czech Resistance*. Baton Rouge: Louisiana State University Press, 2002.

FOR FURTHER READING

BOOKS

Agnew, Hugh LeCaine. *The Czechs and the Lands of the Bohemian Crown.* Stanford, CA: Hoover Institution Press, 2004.

Albright, Madeleine. *Prague Winter: A Personal Story of Remembrance and War, 1937-1948.* New York: HarperCollins, 2012.

Bazant, Jan, Nina Bazantova, and Frances Starn, eds. *The Czech Reader: History, Culture, Politics.* Durham, NC: Duke University Press, 2010.

Binet, Laurent. *HHhH.* New York: Farrar, Straus and Giroux, 2012.

Bouska, Tomáš and Klára Pinerová. *Czechoslovak Political Prisoners: Life Stories of 5 Male and 5 Female Victims of Stalinism.* [Česko: Tomáš Bouska], 2009.

Bryant, Chad. *Prague in Black: Nazi Rule and Czech Nationalism.* Cambridge, MA: Harvard University Press, 2007.

Burian, Michael, et al. *Assassination: Operation Anthropoid, 1941-1942.* Prague: Ministry of Defence of the Czech Republic, 2002.

Faber, David. *Munich, 1938: Appeasement and World War II.* New York: Simon & Schuster, 2008.

Foot, M.R.D. *Resistance: European Resistance to Nazism, 1940-45.* New York: McGraw-Hill, 1997.

Gerwarth, Robert. *Hitler's Hangman: The Life of Heydrich*. New Haven, CT: Yale University Press, 2011.

Ginz, Petr. *The Diary of Petr Ginz, 1941-1942*. New York: Atlantic Monthly Press, 2007.

Grant Duff, Shiela. *Europe and the Czechs*. Harmondsworth, Middlesex, England: Penguin Books Limited, 1938.

Grant Duff, Shiela. *A German Protectorate: The Czechs Under Nazi Rule*. London: Macmillan & Company, 1942.

Heimann, Mary. *Czechoslovakia: The State That Failed*. New Haven, CT: Yale University Press, 2009.

Hurka, Joseph. *Fields of Light: A Son Remembers His Heroic Father*. Wainscott, NY: Pushcart Press, 2001.

Ivanov, Miroslav. *The Assasination of Heydrich, 27 May 1942*. London: Hart-Davis, MacGibbon, 1972.

Kirschbaum, Stanislav. *A History of Slovakia: The Struggle for Survival.*, 2nd ed., New York: Palgrave Macmillian, 2005.

Korbel, Josef. *The Communist Subversion of Czechoslovakia, 1938-1948; The Failure of Coexistence*. Princeton, NJ: Princeton University Press, 1959.

Lukes, Igor. *Czechoslovakia Between Stalin and Hitler: The Diplomacy of Edvard Beneš in the 1930s*. New York: Oxford University Press, 1996.

Luza, Radomir with Christina Vella. *The Hitler Kiss: A Memoir of the Czech Resistance*. Baton Rouge: Louisiana State University Press, 2002.

MacDonogh, Giles. *1938: Hitler's Gamble*. New York: Basic Books, 2009.

Mamatey, Victor S. and Radomir Luza, eds. *A History of the Czechoslovak Republic 1918-1948*. Princeton, NJ: Princeton University Press, 1973.

Martin, John. *The Mirror Caught the Sun: Operation Anthropoid 1942*. [Great Britain]: John Martin, 2009.

Masaryk, Tomáš Garrigue. *The Ideals of Humanity and How to Work*. London: George Allen & Unwin Ltd., 1938.

Mastny, Vojtech. *The Czechs Under Nazi Rule: The Failure of National Resistance, 1939-1942*. New York: Columbia University Press, 1971.

Moravec, František. *Master of Spies: The Memoirs of General František Moravec*. New York: Doubleday, 1975.

Rothkirchen, Livia. *The Jews of Bohemia & Moravia: Facing the Holocaust*. Lincoln: University of Nebraska Press and Jerusalem: Yad Vashem, 2005.

Slouka, Mark. *The Visible World: A Novel*. Boston, MA: Houghton Mifflin Company, 2007.

Waller, John H. *The Unseen War in Europe: Espionage and Conspiracy in the Second World War*. New York: Random House, 1996.

White, Lewis M., Editor. *On All Fronts: Czechoslovaks in World War II*. Boulder: East European Monographs, 1991.

———*On All Fronts: Czechoslovaks in World War II*. Boulder: East European Monographs, 1998.

———*On All Fronts: Czechoslovaks in World War II*. Boulder: East European Monographs, 2000.

INTERNET

"Communist Terror in Czechoslovakia & Anti-Communist Resistance." Veronika Valdova. http://www.anticomm.co.uk. 2012.

"Documenting the People Executed on Political Grounds in the Years, 1948-1989, Josef Robotká (1906-1952)," Institute for the Study of Totalitarian Regimes, http://www.ustrcr.cz/en/josef-robotka-en. 2012.

Pinerová, Klára, "The Interview with Vlasta Jakubová," recorded in Brno, August 17, 2008 and July 7, 2009. The interview is archived in the Oral History Center (COH) in Prague and was also published on the website http://www.politictivezni.cz/http://www.politicalprisoners. eu. 2012.

Political Prisoners.eu. Politicti Vvezni. Political Prisoners. http:// www.politictivezni.cz/http://www.politicalprisoners.eu. 2012.

Šmelová, Ivana, "Osudy politických vezenkyn v letech 1948-1960 [online]/The Life of Female Political Prisoners Between 1948 and 1960." (Diplomová Práce Masarykova Univerzita, Filozofická Fakulta, 2007) 12-19, http://is.muni.cz/th/65117/ff_m/Diplomova_prace.pdf.

Ústav Pro Studium Totalitnich Režimů. Institute for the Study of Totalitarian Regimes. http://www.ustrcr.cz/en. 2012.

Ústav Pamäti Národa. Nation's Memory Institute. http://www.upn. gov.sk/english. 2012.

ACKNOWLEDGMENTS

C HARLES' MANUSCRIPT, COMPLETED in 2007 contained these acknowledgments:

"I thank the following people for helping me along with their encouragement, critical reading, and making my writing read like English. In order of their arrival during my memoir writing process are: my lovely and devoted wife Sandra, my close friend Electra Stamelos, my writing colleague Lori Goff, my dedicated nephew Zachary Poprafsky, my capable editor and niece Lia Fisher-Janosz, and my professors at the University of Michigan-Dearborn: Dr. John Kotre, Dr. Gerald Moran, Dr. Sidney Bolkosky, and Dr. Jonathan Smith. Finally, I wouldn't have been able to organize or maintain my manuscript computer files without the help of my son Gene Novacek."

SINCE CHARLES' DEATH I have worked with many other people who have made this project possible and I wish to thank them. I know Charles would want to thank them also, for without their help the book could not have been published.

I echo Charles' acknowledgment of Lia Fisher-Janosz for her care and expertise. Lia (our first editor) unselfishly took the time to read, edit, and as Charles said "make the manuscript read like English."

I thank Tekla Miller for her support and inspiration, Mary Rapas for offering encouragement and suggestions in the early days of the project after Charles'death, and Elizabeth Testa for her help with the biographies and timeline.

I gratefully acknowledge and thank Nancy Yuktonis Solak for her ongoing help with editing the manuscript and her generous sharing of her knowledge of the self-publishing process.

In the Czech Republic I've been aided immensely with encouragement and translations from my dear friend Jaroslava Patloková and her English student Ondrej Kalenský. I am thankful for the cooperation of Klára Pinerová, fieldworker for Political Prisoners.eu, a Czech-based oral history project which captures and preserves the stories of individuals during the Stalinist era and for the cooperation of Daniel Herman, Director of The Institute for the Study of Totalitarian Regimes.

I am very appreciative of and eternally grateful to my two sisters and friend: Connie Fisher, Nancy Poprafsky, and Linda Wallace who listened, comforted, and offered helpful suggestions on the project at all hours of the night and day.

And Charles, in the stars, for trusting me to be your partner on this project and in life, my love and gratitude for everything.

SANDRA A. NOVACEK
2012

ABOUT THE AUTHOR

CHARLES NOVACEK WAS born in Ožd'any, Czechoslovakia, on May 11, 1928. He graduated from the Industrial College of Engineering in Brno, Czechoslovakia, with a degree in mechanical engineering and attended the Masaryk University School of Law in Brno. After escaping his homeland in 1948, Novacek fled to Germany, then Venezuela and was finally able to immigrate with his family to the United States in 1956 where he taught himself English as his seventh language.

Novacek was a registered professional engineer and spent thirty-three years in the Detroit, Michigan, metropolitan area as a civil engineer, project, design, and quality assurance manager. In retirement Novacek studied Mandarin Chinese and earned a B.G.S and an M.A. in Liberal Studies from the University of Michigan-Dearborn and an M.A. in Painting from Eastern Michigan University.

Novacek wrote and painted all of his life, but didn't start writing his memoir, *Border Crossings: Coming of Age in the Czech Resistance*, until the year 2000. He died in July 2007.

CPSIA information can be obtained at www.ICGtesting.com
Printed in the USA
BVOW08s1950130815

413318BV00002B/25/P